A COMPTON-BURNETT
COMPENDIUM

BY VIOLET POWELL

Five out of Six
A Substantial Ghost
The Irish Cousins
A Compton-Burnett Compendium

A Compton-Burnett Compendium

Violet Powell

HEINEMANN: LONDON

William Heinemann Ltd
15 Queen Street, Mayfair, London W1X 8BE

LONDON MELBOURNE TORONTO
JOHANNESBURG AUCKLAND

First published in Great Britain 1973
Copyright © by Violet Powell 1973
SBN: 434 59954 9

Printed in Great Britain by
Western Printing Services Ltd, Bristol

For John

Contents

Biographical Note

Ivy Compton-Burnett was born at Pinner on June 5th, 1884. She was sixth in the family of twelve children born to Doctor James Compton Burnett, and the eldest child of his second marriage. She was educated at the Addiscombe College for the Daughters of Gentlemen, Hove, Sussex, and at the Royal Holloway College, Egham, Surrey. For thirty years, until Miss Margaret Jourdain's death in 1951, Dame Ivy shared her home with this well-known expert on Regency furniture. In 1951 Ivy Compton-Burnett received a C.B.E. in recognition of her contribution to literature. She was created a D.B.E. in 1967. She died in London on August 27th, 1969.

List of Novels and Dates of Original Publication

Introduction with Acknowledgements

There could be no better description of the novels of Dame
Ivy Compton-Burnett than the words used by Jane Austen
at the end of Chapter V in *Northanger Abbey*. Having
written that 'there seems almost a general wish of decrying
the capacity and undervaluing the labour of the novelist,
and of slighting the performances which have only genius,
wit and taste to recommend them', Miss Austen proceeds to
castigate those who smugly deny that they ever read such
frivolous works, or who, if detected in doing so, excuse themselves with the words, ' "Oh! It is only a novel" '. Or, as
Miss Austen goes on to say, 'Only some work in which the
greatest powers of the human mind are displayed, in which
the most thorough knowledge of human nature, the happiest
delineation of its varieties, the liveliest effusions of wit and
humour are conveyed to the world in the best chosen
language.'

Those well-read in Dame Ivy's works will agree that this
summing-up is peculiarly applicable. Those with this pleasure
still to come may, by these words, be stimulated to discover
for themselves the fascination of the Compton-Burnett world.
To both categories of readers it is hoped that this Compendium
will provide a scenic view of a body of work of which the
genius, wit and taste increases the more it is explored.

I must thank Messrs Victor Gollancz for permission to
quote from all Dame Ivy's novels published since 1925. I
must also thank Messrs Blackwood to quote from *Dolores*,
first published by them in 1911 and re-issued in 1971. I am
much obliged to Messrs Hamish Hamilton for permission to

quote from *Saint-Simon at Versailles* (edited and translated by Lucy Norton, 1958). Dame Ivy's views on *The Real Charlotte* (p. 100) were expressed in a letter to myself.

In addition I am deeply grateful to my friends Sonia Orwell and Hilary Spurling, the former for encouraging me in a friendship with Dame Ivy in the last years of her life, and the latter for generous help in matters of biographical detail. I must also thank my husband, Anthony Powell, for his help and patience during a period of work which seemed, at times, likely to be extended to infinity.

Violet Powell

1

THE FIRST STEP

In considering the novels of I. Compton-Burnett, it is the first step that encounters the most formidable stumbling-block. She began her writing career in 1911 with a novel called *Dolores*, using her full name of Ivy Compton-Burnett. Like a hopelessly delinquent child, this book was subsequently disowned by its author. When, fourteen years later, she wrote *Pastors and Masters* the book appeared as by I. Compton-Burnett, the form of her name which she made famous. The guillotine of the First World War had cut short the life of her most loved brother, and the effect on Compton-Burnett's literary development was almost equally violent. She pruned her style remorselessly, banishing from her work, at the same time, many aspects of everyday life, which she preferred to ignore or to consider irrelevant for her creative purposes. It is therefore a problem as to whether *Dolores* should be ignored as a false step or treated as worthy of study on account of the passages which came to perfection in later novels. Although the book is burdened with surplus literary baggage, to dismiss *Dolores* as unworthy of attention would be to lose an opportunity to understand the strong technical discipline by which Compton-Burnett achieved her later purity of narrative style.

'An open grave with its mourners. It is a daily thing but not to be denied our need. Let us mark the figure foremost in the sombre throng, that clerical figure of heavy build and bent head. That is the Reverend Cleveland Hutton, the vicar of the parish.' After this extract from the first page of *Dolores*, the book proceeds for fifteen more pages in the same tone of voice, dreeing the weird at the burial of the Reverend Cleveland Hutton's wife. She has left behind her a daughter, Dolores, whose professional and emotional martyrdom is the suitably sorrowful theme of the book. Mr Hutton marries, again and adds three more children to his family, children who require a governess. Dolores, plain but clever, is obliged to sacrifice her university scholarship to fill this post, unpaid. This sacrifice also involves abandoning her rôle as pupil and assistant to Claverhouse, a gloomy, impoverished writer of classical dramas. Some improvement in her family's fortunes allows Dolores to return to her college, but in the interval Claverhouse (although nearly blind he has a doubtlessly foolish prejudice in favour of good looks) falls in love with Perdita, a pretty friend of Dolores'. In a further exercise of mistaken self-sacrifice, Dolores forwards the marriage by revealing to Perdita that Dolores' brother Bertram, between whom and Perdita there is an attraction, is already secretly married. As Dolores' passion for Claverhouse is equalled by her passion for Perdita their marriage is a two-pronged agony to her. After nine uncomfortable months, the birth of a still-born child brings Perdita's life to an end, and Dolores returns to the task of helping Claverhouse in his blindness. But her stepmother soon puts a stop to that by dying bequeathing on her deathbed the care of the family to Dolores. Dolores' sacrifice again becomes superfluous, for her father marries for the third time. Soulsby, a good kind don, who has been urging Dolores to solve her problems by marrying him, takes one look at Sophia, Dolores' beautiful half-sister, and changes his inclination. Although prevented from being in time to interpret Claverhouse's last blind efforts to release his genius.

Dolores is, at last, able to rejoin her college senior common-room. The book ends with her colleagues discussing the self-consciousness of those who have received and refused proposals of marriage.

' "Miss Hutton, can you meet our eyes?" said Miss Adam, not without suggestion that this was beyond herself.

"Oh, we will acquit Miss Hutton. She is the most sensible of us all," said Miss Cliff.'

Even from these brief quotations it will be clear that *Dolores* ends on a vastly different note than that struck at its beginning. It is not, however, until the last few pages that the turgidity of the style suddenly clarifies, and the reader is presented with a scene which contains the germ of the common-room scenes in *More Women than Men*, a book written twenty years later. Otherwise there are long passages of gothic horror, when Claverhouse's ancient mother and a witch-like maid-servant struggle with the discomforts of a ramshackle house in an Oxford back street.

When, after his mother's death, Claverhouse brings home Perdita as his bride, the couple are described as lying side by side in bed, but their unease is such that to read, later, of Perdita's death in childbirth is almost a surprise. Incidentally, though pregnancies, legitimate and illegitimate, play an important part in many Compton-Burnett novels, this is the only occasion on which she attempted to describe normal physical relations between the sexes. Even allowing for the euphemisms of the period, the effort is unconvincing. Wisely, in later books, conception takes place off-stage. Another line of description which was to be abandoned is detailed analysis of religious organizations, such as those that operated in the Reverend Cleveland Hutton's parish. Besides this High Anglican vicar, there is a Wesleyan Minister, and the latter's chief adherent, a proselytising teetotaler, who compensates for failure to enter Parliament by missionary activity.

3

Additionally, there is the local doctor, whose horror of any taint of Roman Catholicism makes his relationship with the vicar a matter of delicacy. Although clergymen occur in the following six of I. Compton-Burnett's novels, little is made of their doctrine or ritualistic practices, except for Eustace Bellamy (*Men and Wives*) who appears to have a taste for dressing himself as what W. S. Gilbert described as an 'ecclesiastical Guy Fawkes'. It is the private characters rather than the public practices of the clergy which are laid before the reader. Another passage from *Dolores* which has an echo in a later book is to be found in the skirmish between the second Mrs Hutton and her sister Mrs Blackwood, wife of the teetotal Wesleyan.

' "I remember you so well when you were engaged," said Mrs Hutton, with a little laugh.

"I remember it too," said Mrs Blackwood; "and how I used to pity you, for having no chance of getting married, though you were the elder sister. Girls are so amusing in the way they look at things." ' This exchange is a cruder version of the cut and thrust between Matty Seaton and her sister Blanche in *A Family and a Fortune*. Mrs Blackwood, like Matty Seaton being left in the possession of the field by the death of her opponent.

The perpetually sacrificed Dolores is still only in her thirties when she finally comes to rest in the senior common-room from which home duties had so frequently called her. With a predeliction for heroines and villainesses of riper years, I. Compton-Burnett could well have resurrected Dolores in a later incarnation, but when she began, twelve years later, to deal once again with university life, extremes of self-sacrifice had gone overboard among the surplus corded bales of her earliest literary style.

4

2

THESE DONS AND PEOPLE

' "Well this is a nice thing! A nice thing this schoolmastering!
Up at seven, and in a room with a black fire . . . And while
you are about it, don't pile on as much coal as it would take
the day's profits of the school to pay for." '

In this opening paragraph to *Pastors and Masters* the
pattern is set for many subsequent first chapters. The author
had an eminently reasonable prejudice for beginning a novel
at the beginning of the day. In fact, eleven of her twenty
novels begin with the members of a family assembled for
their first meal. This is frequently preceded by prayers,
a wise precaution, as in many cases the need for a message
of peace and love is acute.

Mr Merry, quoted above, has his forty scholars as well as
his own family's spiritual welfare to consider. Throughout
Pastors and Masters the boys are treated with a mixture of
abuse and servility by their preceptor, while the boys themselves are both chorus and backcloth. Comments on the habits
of their teachers, and the stinginess of the house-keeping,
illuminate the lives of their elders rather than their own.
Before the grey tones of this frieze of hobgoblins, the pastors
and masters, with their females, act out a drama of literary
and sexual intrigue.

Mr Merry does the work of the school, with the assistance
of Mrs Merry (Scripture) Miss Basden (matron, music and

French) and Mr Burgess (other subjects). All are slightly afraid of each other, and only unusual exasperation leads them to defend themselves by snapping. The owner of the school, Mr Herrick, descends like Zeus from Olympus, to read prayers, and then retreats to the comfort of his own quarters, and to the company of his half-sister Emily who presides there. Mr Merry's qualification for partnership in this academy is personal rather than academic. His ability to switch on a tender charm of manner is irresistible to anxious or prospective parents, a gift accepted by Mr Herrick as an unacknowledged but important contribution to the financial success of the school.

Nicholas Herrick is seventy years old, his half-sister Emily twenty years younger. She has the face of 'an attractive idol', and her caressingly feline manner suggests that this might well be a cat-headed goddess. Two friends, William Masson and Richard Bumpus, come between the brother and sister in age, being also Fellows of the same college as Herrick, a barely materialised college in a shadowy university. With Herrick, these two dons have watched beside the death-bed of an older colleague, a vigil which seems to have released creative forces in the watchers. It becomes apparent that Herrick, after a working life of criticism has at last got the scheme of an original work clear in his mind. Bumpus, having in youth buried his only novel in the grave of a friend, has now completed a more mature book. Both men are intensely desirous of belated literary success.

' "Real books coming out of our own heads!" said Bumpus, "And not just printed unkindness to other people's." '

Their talk moves on to the nature of God.

' "Are we going to be broad and wicked?" said Emily.'

In later novels the broadness and wickedness usually comes from younger sceptics, raising incensed protest from their elders. Here it is the elders who build up a picture of a deity, 'grasping and fond of praise', 'superior, vindictive and over-indulgent'. Herrick, as the part-owner of a school for young boys, makes a far from strong protest, and Bumpus praises Herrick for his quiet conscientiousness in being behind the parents' backs what he would be to their faces if he ever happened to see them.

' "I am deeply grateful to Merry," said Herrick. "Nobody knows what seeing them is." '

Emily's female confidant is Theresa Fletcher, the old wife of yet another old pastor, whose household is further depressed by a young nephew, also in holy orders, and a sister who devotes herself to the poor, particularly the male poor. It has been explained that Masson and Bumpus 'had meant romance to each other in youth'. With the uncomfortable avenue of a solitary old age beginning to open before Emily, Theresa Fletcher urges her to consider that she might marry William Masson. Emily agrees that she could arrange to propose to William, who would certainly be too considerate not to accept her, but gives a temperate answer to Theresa's suggestion that William does want to marry her friend.

' "As much as he can want to marry anyone. Anyone who is a woman. And that is not very much."

"Oh dear! These dons and people!" said Theresa.'

Emily goes on to imply that she also prefers her own sex, aware that Theresa knows that already. Emily adds that she understands why people sometimes murder those to whom they are attached, and she thinks it right for them to do so. Indications have also been given that Theresa's husband, the Reverend Peter Fletcher, might be classed emotionally, with what his wife calls 'these dons and people'.

An explicit statement of an attraction towards one's own sex would be less remarkable if *Pastors and Masters* had not appeared in 1925. Three years later Radclyffe Hall, in *The Well of Loneliness*, developed in a turgid volume a sexual attitude which Compton-Burnett had expressed in a few neat paragraphs. *The Well of Loneliness* raised a gale of moral and legal condemnation which blustered for years, while *Pastors and Masters* remained uncensured. Neither was there a public outcry against *More Women than Men* (1933) which explores a pattern of relationships that change from homosexual to heterosexual and vice versa. The still, small, voice of calm in which Compton-Burnett habitually wrote of perverted habits gave her protection from the attacks which brought more violent writers into the toils of legal processes.

To return to Mr Merry's school, the preparations for prize-giving provide the headmaster with an opportunity to juggle nervously with his varied professional problems. His display of virtuosity includes a simultaneous harrying of his pupils, attempts to placate his wife and stoking a smouldering warfare with his male assistant. Mr Merry is to make a speech after the prizes have been presented, though Masson objects that it is not the schoolmaster's business to praise his own school.

' "You thought Merry's business was not that?" said Bumpus. "Then what did you think his business was?" '

Mr Merry's speech, and indeed his demeanour throughout the prize-giving, is an extension of his juggling act, assuaging the disappointed feelings of parents whose children have won no prizes, and glossing over the fact that the strain of the occasion has reduced Mrs Merry to tears. Introduced in the course prize-giving are Mr Bentley and his daughter. The two Bentley sons are among Mr Merry's non-prize-winning pupils. Mr Bentley, yet another pastor, has heard of Mr Herrick's book, and inquires if its subject is likely to be of interest—he means of educational use—to the boys. Steering nimbly round this awkward question, Mr Merry expatiates on the subtle atmosphere of culture generated by Mr Herrick's

literary efforts, even if these are not written for boyish understanding.

Mr Bentley has little importance in the plot of *Pastors and
Masters*, but he is significant as an early sketch in a portrait
gallery of fathers and grandfathers. In his domestic behaviour
there are hints which are picked out and developed in later
books. Something of Duncan Edgeworth (*A House and its
Head*) can be remarked in Mr Bentley's bullying complaints
at his family's lateness for breakfast. His deep, and not ill-
founded, suspicion that his sons' education will hardly fit
them for earning their bread, is shared, in even greater depth,
by a father in *A Heritage and its History*, and by a grandfather in *Parents and Children*. A slight ailment of one of his
sons gives Mr Bentley an opportunity to change his plans for
his own convenience, at the same time threatening his
daughter with the prospect of her brother's death as a result
of her neglect. Persisting in his emotional stir-up, he reduces
his other son to tears by painting a grisly picture of the boy's
future remorse, when his father has sunk to the grave under
the burden of an ungrateful family. Unlike some of the later
Compton-Burnett parental bullies, Mr Bentley is granted no
charm and no pathos, but he is allowed the judgement necessary to sum up Mr Merry's failings, with an accuracy born of
discontent at Merry's scholastic methods.

' "I was thinking of Merry being such an unmitigated nin-
compoop. Such talk as his no sane man would credit . . . It is
enough to ruin a boy to listen to it." ' That this criticism can
be accepted by the reader as totally just is a measure of the
success of Mr Merry's portrait.

Cold winds blow through the cracks in the house of friendship when the Herricks, Bumpus and Masson assemble, so that
Herrick and Bumpus may read aloud the book that each has
recently completed. The group parts with the books still
unread. It has been revealed, obliquely, that Herrick's book

is the same as Bumpus' book, and that this book is no new work, but the regurgitation of an early volume, buried, Rossetti-like, in the grave of a loved friend. In the course of the death-bed watch beside old Crabbe, Bumpus had left his manuscript in Crabbe's study. Herrick, during his share of the vigil, has, it appears, purloined the book, under the impression that it had been written by Crabbe, and was therefore unknown and ownerless. The imminence of a show-down which will exhibit Herrick as a literary thief, and Bumpus as a poseur, unwilling to carry through with a romantic gesture, is averted by the quick kindness of the faithful Masson. Bumpus, Masson realizes, has been led into this petty deception by a gnawing desire for literary recognition. Herrick, poised on the edge of an even more humiliating exposure, skips back from the brink with agility, his retreat being covered by Emily's adroit small talk. So smoothly goes this manoeuvre that Herrick, his own book safely burnt, regains his confidence in his intellectual impregnability. Soon he is able to refer to Bumpus as ' "My dear old gifted, erring friend." '

The thwarted literary ambitions of the professors, the anxieties of the headmaster, and the disgruntlement of the father with his unsympathetic family are gathered together in a dinner party at which everyone is wonderfully like themselves. The author takes this opportunity to let the guests speak on the subject of their favourite reading matter, a question passed round the company in the manner of the sixpence in the game of Up Jenkins. I. Compton-Burnett had no illusions as to the opinions held by such critics as the Reverend Francis Fletcher, most egregious of the pastors, on what he describes as books ' "written by ladies for ladies" '. Excusing thus his neglect of Jane Austen, Francis Fletcher announces that The Book is his principal study. Anxious to impress him, Miss Delia Bentley hastens to add that it is also hers. Miss Lydia Fletcher, the philanthropist, declares that she only reads history, while Miss Basden (matron and French) insists that she prefers to read any language except English. Herrick takes an even more extreme stand.

' "I am one of the greatest readers alive" . . . "I have read all European modern literature, the enormous bulk of it. And I have read as much medieval literature as any man living." ' After this stupendous claim, it is entirely suitable that the book should end with Herrick's reflection that he does not think he has ever been on ' "the ordinary line," ' his sister Emily replying, ' "No, I am sure you have not. It would have been dreadful of you." '

In its style *Pastors and Masters* reflects the stark mood of the nineteen twenties, superfluous description being peeled away, until the skeleton of story has only dialogue to clothe its bare bones. Extreme in its anti-Dickensianism, the outline of the school is only slightly less pale than the lines which sketch the university background. Such domestic squalors as the underground dining-room, and the watery marmalade offered to the boys in this catacomb, are details chosen to illustrate character and situation, rather than to provide the grisly drama created by the administration of brimstone and treacle at Dotheboys Hall. Compton-Burnett had already mastered her special technique of stating simply the initial predicament of her characters, reserving their own thoughts and speech for later phases of the story, when hearts are opened and confidences come to painful birth.

3

PARENTS AND POSSESSORS

Brothers and Sisters followed *Pastors and Masters* in 1929, and stylistically, moved away from the plainness of its predecessor, though resembling it in having patterns of event and personality which were to be developed in later novels. The difficulties in which the characters from *Brothers and Sisters* find themselves are due, principally, to the overweening pride of Andrew Stace, a patriarch of a type from whose loins Compton-Burnett families frequently have the misfortune to spring. Andrew's boast, 'that no man had ever despised him and that no man had ever broken him in', prevents him from being able to admit that the adopted son he has brought up is, in reality, his own child, and so disqualified from marrying his legitimate daughter. Leaving a letter which explains matters, Andrew dies. His daughter Sophia, already pledged to Christian, whom she knows only as her father's adopted son, believes that the letter contains no more than a will disinheriting Christian and herself should they marry. With a reasonable regard for her worldly prospects she conceals the letter in a locked desk. Her dead father's apparently irrational objection to the marriage of Christian and Sophia is only known to Miss Patmore, the first of I. Compton-Burnett's studies of female companions, domestic victims of the moods of their employers and unable to escape from a net woven by love and custom.

The story of *Brothers and Sisters* then bounds forward to the twenty-fifth birthday of Andrew, eldest son of Christian and Sophia Stace. Victims of their mother's egotism, Andrew, Dinah his sister and Robin his brother lead a life in which truth has been sacrificed to the expediency of feeding Sophia's appetite for admiration. Their father, his health overstrained by his medical work, has never turned his mind to consider the burden that his wife lays on their children. Miss Patmore, alone, supplies undemanding love and a safe port in domestic storms, her only weakness being a devouring curiosity about every detail of the family to which she has dedicated her life. In due course there is plenty for her curiosity to devour.

In an attempt to limit the size of Andrew's birthday dinner-party, Sophia has invited Peter Bateman a cousin, his daughter Tilly and his son Latimer merely to have a cup of tea. Peter Bateman is poor as a relation, and also poor as a doctor compared with Christian Stace, but he is adroit enough at social manoeuvring to compel Sophia to add the three Batemans to the dinner-party. Peter's insensitiveness makes him unaware that his children suffer continual humiliation from their poverty and lack of prospects, a suffering increased by their father's jocular references to the oddity of his children's appearance, and the impossibility of their rich, handsome cousins considering them as a potential husband or wife.

Two more pairs of brothers and sisters attend the dinner party, Edward Dryden, rector of the parish, who has an 'old worldness that allowed him the church as a provision for his sister (Judith) and himself', and Sarah and Julian Wake, who 'were reputed to be very devoted and very well off, and enjoyed even more prosperity and mutual affection than was said'. As the company moves into dinner, Dinah says that it would be absurd to say that prayer was answered, for in that case Latimer, obliged by a lack of female partners to go in on his father's arm, would have been struck dead on his way to the dining-room. New settlers in the village are discussed, a Frenchwoman called Mrs Lang, her son Gilbert and her daughter Caroline. This family brings with it a cyclone of revelation, which leaves behind it a trail of shattered reputations and blasted romances.

Gilbert and Caroline Lang become engaged to Dinah and Andrew Stace, but some early photographs, innocently produced by Patty, reveal to Mrs Lang that Christian Stace is her son. Consequently her children are uncle and aunt, by half-blood, to their chosen mates. Mrs Lang calls off the marriages in an interview with Christian, but dies without telling him who his father had been. The survivors face the fact that there has been a narrow escape from involuntary incest. Not everyone has escaped this predicament. As Christian's health gets worse, Sophia develops a superstitious dread that there is a curse on the family because, after her father's death, she neglected his command to open a certain desk. Burying in the back of her mind the suspicion that a will disinheriting Christian and herself should they marry is still in existence, she has kept the key of the desk in which this time-bomb is ticking on her key-ring, though taking the precaution of maintaining that it has been lost.

Prompted by Sophia, Christian goes alone to open the desk. He suffers a shock that is mortal on finding not a will (the reader knows that this has been destroyed) but a letter which tells Christian that he is Andrew Stace's natural son, and so has married his half-sister. Always on the alert from love and curiosity, Miss Patmore finds him dead, and reads the letter, 'with her look of grief and terror conquered by a yearning as fierce'. Before fetching help, she locks the desk with its lethal secret inside, and for a while she alone knows that it was not the effort of mounting the stairs that precipitated Christian's heart failure.

Sophia does not make her widowhood easy for her children. A second double engagement between Dinah and Andrew and Edward, the clergyman, and Judith, his sister, is treated by Sophia as something that has no importance except as it concerns herself. She has, it turns out, some reason for this attitude, for, when faced by yet another revelation of a moral lapse and its consequences, Edward and Judith show terror without pity. Herself now faced with mortal sickness, Sophia once again arranges for the desk to be opened and this time it is Andrew who has the shock of reading the letter. From Sophia's reaction, her children learn that she has lived with the belief that she has concealed an inconvenient will throughout the span of their lives together, and that this illegal act has in no way influenced her view of herself as possessing transcendentally magnificent qualities.

Fading into the last stages of her illness, Sophia is unable to control her words, and reveals the incestuous secret to Peter Bateman, her medical attendant. Edward's shock at finding that his future wife and future brother-in-law will be widely known to have only half the conventional number of grandfathers leads him to suggest that the dying Sophia should be segregated, with the unreal hope that Peter can be silenced. His sister Judith supports him in his inhumanity, and their attitude results in a breaking of the engagements by the appalled Staces. Sophia accepts this breach without being aware that she is responsible, referring to the dismissed couple as rather 'shallow', to the pleasure of her son Robin. Not being emotionally involved, Robin can also only rejoice at his sister's remorseless attack on her former fiancé, which includes the remark that she will not offer to be Edward's sister, ' "because in our family that seems to lead to marriage." '

Finally, there is a general retreat to London, a clearing of the stage which finds no place in later Compton-Burnett finales. Peter, his son, the tortured Latimer, and his daughter Tilly, are left alone in the village, where Tilly has found a husband, described by her father as ' "the little house agent; he isn't such a bad little fellow." ' Peter contemplates the new family who will replace the Staces at the Manor with exhilarated feelings.

' "It will mean a new life for us. People have to get to know their doctor."

"Yes. They will not be able to help it," said Latimer.'

Brothers and Sisters marks the end of what may be called the introductory, or experimental phase, of Compton-Burnett's novels. In *Pastors and Masters* she had written with a bareness of style, minor characters being faintly indicated in the background. The cast of *Brothers and Sisters* is, however, far more clearly defined. The Staces have the moments of greatest drama, but the Langs and the Wakes are given their full share of dialogue, and, as there is no apparent blood relation in question, they are ultimately able to achieve that double marriage which kinship and rancour has prevented among their neighbours. On the other hand, Andrew Stace, Sophia's father, is set before the reader with such force that there is a sense of loss when, after twenty pages he takes his spiritual arrogance to meet a Maker whom he himself regarded as likely to consider his, Andrew's, creation an 'outstanding piece of work'. No other character, not even Sophia at the apex of her domination, comes across as clearly as her father, spilling his wine from a tremor of old age, 'and frowning with no less bitterness against old age, that he had taken every care to attain it'. Christian, the upright, hard-working man is not a portrait that the author attempted to repeat. Sophia's characteristics, on the other hand, reappear in many subsequent female portraits, sometimes in a grandmother, sometimes in a mother, and, on occasion, in an unmarried aunt, the term maiden being grotesquely unsuitable to such characters as Matilda Seaton in *A Family and a Fortune*, or Hetta Ponsonby in *Daughters and Sons*. Miss Patmore is the forerunner of a succession of companions, uneasily situated between the gentlefolk and their domestics, sometimes transformed from governesses and sometimes changing into them, but in most cases their only reward for suffering the exactions of their employers being the delight of a furtively satisfied curiosity.

Edward Dryden, the rector, is less starkly unpleasant than Mr Bentley, and less sanctimonious that the Reverend Francis Fletcher, clerics who appear in *Pastors and Masters*. Unlike the Reverend Peter Fletcher his sexual tastes would seem impeccably normal, but Edward is revealed as possessing a soul devoid of pity or nobility. (Bishops never appear among Compton-Burnett clerical portraits, and this is hardly surprising if the queer fish they would be called upon to ordain are considered.) By now the author had laid the foundations of the world she was to make peculiarly her own, whose inhabitants were to be her subjects in both senses of the word. The frontiers had become fixed, though children, domestic servants, baronets and solicitors were to be added to the inhabitants, and it would be well to examine the depths and limits of this territory, which its creator was to explore and probe with a mastery both subtle and unrelenting.

4

HOUSES, PROFESSIONS
AND OCCUPATIONS

The world of I. Compton-Burnett's novels has its roots in the English countryside of the eighteen-eighties, a date, in at least one case, being given in a speech by a leading character. The inimitable Sir Godfrey Haslam (*Men and Wives*) fixes the year as 1889 by giving the date of his arrival in his house and then by asking Buttermere, his butler, to agree that he would never take his employer for a man of fifty-six. Buttermere's response to this appeal is as unyielding in its disobligingness as his demeanour throughout the book.

' "Well, what would you say, Buttermere?"

"Good morning, Sir Godfrey," Buttermere said.'

An even more precise date is given at the opening of *A House and Its Head*, which begins on Christmas Day 1885. But in neither of these books does the author appear to have hesitated when she found an anachronism necessary to the progress of her story, superbly ignoring any anomaly that may have arisen in consequence. The divorce laws of the nineteen-thirties are back-dated to the eighteen-eighties, taking with them the custom that a woman could escape the stigma of adulteress if the husband agreed to be the guilty party. In addition the Reverend Ernest Bellamy, the rector in *Men and Wives*, has no difficulty in divorcing the bitch-hearted but irresistible Camilla, retaining his living, and marrying again.

Another anachronistic quirk occurs in *More Women than Men*, when Felix Bacon, called to the telephone to hear the disapproval of his father, Sir Robert, of his son's proposal to teach drawing in a girls' school, refuses a second allowance of minutes, commends the cleverness that had hit on the amount that ' "just gets every thing in!" ' This reference to the timing of telephone calls fits ill with a world in which there is no place for the internal combustion engine, travelling by road taking place solely in horse-drawn vehicles.

The carriage folk themselves live in houses that range from stately, but usually dilapidated, mansions, to gate lodges disguised by a semblance of gentility. With the exception of *More Women than Men* where the school buildings are the centre of action, it is the mansions in their varying degrees of grandeur which are the focal points of their own rural neighbourhoods. Financial stringency oppresses most of the landowners, who often enforce Spartan measures of economy, at the same time assuring their hapless descendants that these show gross ingratitude for a life of unearned luxury, for which the workhouse is the only alternative. Best feet are put forward when neighbours are entertained, and the neighbours, having few other engagements, are always avid to assist at the simmering dramas to be observed at the big house.

At dinner parties the dramas are apt to boil over. Harriet Haslam breaks up the evening by an attempt at suicide, subsequently shown to be a self-deception. Sabine Ponsonby (*Daughters and Sons*) goes even further, and actually breathes her last at the dinner table, with singularly little shock to the assembled company, even allowing for the relief of being released from the hostess's unbridled temper. In between the mansions and the lodges there are dwelling-places of varying degrees of comfort. Some, like the home of Doctor Smollet (*A House and Its Head*) are 'small but chosen'. Some are bleak and unloved, like the house to which Simon Challoner is exiled, having thoughtlessly got his uncle's wife with an heir (A *Heritage and Its History*).

The men who live in these houses have a number of professions, but within certain strict bounds of human activity. Those who own land make its care an occupation, without arresting the decline of the land's value, but wishing to pass on the estate to the next male heir. Meanwhile, the heir himself is not infrequently provided with the frustrating career of being supposed to assist in the estate's management. In a variation of Œdipus's doom, not only Simon Challenor, as already mentioned, but Grant Edgeworth (A *House and Its Head*) jeopardise their inheritance by fathering sons who disinherit their progenitors.

Doctors, clergymen and solicitors play important parts in the novels. With the early exception of Peter Bateman (*Brothers and Sisters*) doctors tend to be intelligent and dedicated, though, after arranging for his mother to die by her own hand, it is doubtful if Matthew Haslam (*Men and Wives*) would be an entirely reliable medical adviser in the London practice to which he retreats. Clergymen, as has been seen, are given a rough ride, though no other is painted so blackly as Jonathan Swift (*More Women than Men*). A seducer of both sexes, he is prepared in addition to take the credit for the support of his illegitimate son, support which, in reality, is being earned by the boy's mother. After *Daughters and Sons*, however, where the Reverend Doctor Chaucer proposes to one governess, adds a serious assault to his proposal to another, and finally marries the handsome but fiendish Hetta Ponsonby, clergymen are phased out. They have paid their quit rent and deserve to go in peace.

Solicitors are treated by Compton-Burnett somewhat better than clergymen, but not so well as doctors. Amid examples of foolishness of mind and abuse of professional confidences only Ridley Cranmer (*Parents and Children*) achieves such positive wickedness that he loses his clients. His attempt at a bigamous marriage with a supposed widow, for whom he is trustee, is thwarted, and he takes his revenge by revealing that the patriarch of the family to whom he is legal adviser, has not only a past of sexual incontinence, but a habit of parsimony towards his bastards.

The two other professions open to the inhabitants of the Compton-Burnett world are teaching and the practice of literature. Painting and music, incidentally, are not arts that are practised as professions. Schoolgirls learn to draw, children love to paint, but their talents make no mark in later life. Music is only a subject to be learnt at school, and except in *Two Worlds and Their Ways*, where Oliver Shelley plays the piano, school is where music remains. Teaching, on the other hand, is a career followed by men and women, their proficiency being variable. The staff of Josephine Napier's (*More Women than Men*) school are highly qualified, but Mildred Hallam (*Darkness and Day*) has only self-confidence to recommend her. This is barely a match for the intransigence of her pupils, to whom she happens to be an illegitimate half-sister. Many of the tutors also suffer from bullying by their pupils, an exception being Alfred Marcon (*Daughters and Sons*) whose professional success is vitiated by the ease with which he works himself into a nervous breakdown. Indeed it is surprising that none of the great gallery of governesses arrive at a similar collapse. They give notice on occasion, but this is usually brought on by the diabolical behaviour of their pupils, rather than by the overstrain of their own powers.

The other profession shared by men and women in the Compton-Burnett world is that of literature. Some write ' "real books coming out of our own heads" '. Charity Marcon, the giraffe-like spinster from *Daughters and Sons* has a more detached view of her literary activities. ' " I have been up to London to get the book I am writing out of the British

21

Museum . . . So many people were there getting out their books. It doesn't seem to matter everything's being in books already; I don't mind it at all." ' From the same book, John Ponsonby, a novelist whose popularity is on the wane, is such a figure of continuous defeat that it is difficult to believe that he has had the amount of success with which he is credited. Hereward Egerton (*A God and His Gifts*) is far more credible as a successful writer, his literary drive being equalled by his sexual potency. Together, these carry him through a sequence of seduction and subsequent revelation daunting to a man whose conception of his god-like situation was less complete.

As interesting as the professions and social habits prevalent in the world of Compton-Burnett are the professions that are not followed, and the habits which do not prevail. No one is, or has ever been, in the service of the Crown. Country gentlemen never join the yeomanry. No mention of warfare by land or sea occurs in the conversational marathons customary in Compton-Burnett families. The sons of the house take examinations for which they study in conventional fashion, but they do not obtrude their inevitable knowledge of the battles of history. Jane Austen has been accused of superficiality in largely ignoring the Napoleonic Wars, which were both the background of her life and a threat to her sailor brothers. Whether from reasons of personal suffering at the loss of her own brother, or from the conviction that military activity would be alien in the world she had created, Compton-Burnett went further than Jane Austen. No faint note of a bugle, no rumbling of a distant gun-carriage, disturbs the landscape in which purely domestic campaigns are conducted.

Travel is seldom for pleasure. Visits to foreign countries, or distant continents, are usually undertaken for business so that the author can shake the kaleidoscope of family life. The temporary absence of an important figure allows a new pattern to appear, which is apt to give a shock to the returning traveller.

As has been seen, solicitors play an important part, but their concern is with property, or sometimes with divorce. They have no criminal practice, none of the actual crimes detected being brought even before a magistrate, a service not undertaken by any squire or baronet. Baronets, themselves, constitute a social ceiling above which no one rises, which is again in contrast to Jane Austen, who, dealing largely in baronets, cast occasional glances at the House of Lords. Jane Austen understood the principle, which Evelyn Waugh has described as the fragmentation of the strata of English upper-class life. He gave as an example that a baker's dozen of viscountesses are not found having tea in the drawing-room, while twenty-two baronets play cricket in the park. Viscountesses do not occur in Compton-Burnett drawing-rooms, and no cricket is played in her parks by any of her clutch of baronets, or indeed by anyone else.

Organised games are not permitted to any grown-up or child. At home, croquet hoops and tennis nets are unknown in the gardens, and, though the two eldest sons in *A Family and a Fortune* have passed through Eton, they observe silence on any experiences they may have had on its playing fields. On the other hand I. Compton-Burnett's faultlessly accurate observation of children inspire macabre accounts of the rituals and games that young children evolve for themselves, excuses for a funeral being particularly welcome.

The county assemblies and hunt balls, which might be expected to play their part in settling young ladies in life with suitable husbands, are not frequented, or even mentioned. Consequently the marriages among first cousins (sometimes double) are hardly surprising, though after *Brothers and Sisters* no incestuous marriage occurs. No race meetings are attended by even the more sporting of Compton-Burnett characters. Their fortunes are lost in unwise speculation or extravagance, and not by slow horses or fast women, extra-marital commitments being fulfilled in a niggardly spirit. Reasonably enough, cooks are of considerable importance, though Mrs Lovat (*Darkness and Day*) is exceptionally fortunate in retaining an excellent cook, because she is the devoted but unacknowledged mother of Mrs Lovat's daughter-in-law. There are indications of the menus prepared both for everyday meals and for parties, but, oddly enough, only one picnic takes place. Mellicent and Polly Hardisty return from this with unabated appetites. As they join the family luncheon-table their stepmother Rachel remarks, ' "I thought that was why places were so untidy after picnics, that people took sandwiches and could not eat them. I don't understand why so much is left, if they can be used." ' Rachel is Sir Percy Hardisty's second wife, and in *Men and Wives*, the novel next to be considered, she is a stalwart figure of abrasive good sense among a crowd of egoists and neurotics. As will be seen, Rachel's qualities enable her to bind up the wounds of her friends with one hand, while cutting down their enemies with the other.

5

AN ACQUAINTANCE
WITH CRIME

Plagiarism and will-suppression have already made their appearance in the early novels, when I. Compton-Burnett was working her way towards the literary approach that she was to make so completely her own. With *Men and Wives*, and its two immediate successors, mere violation of the Law gives way to blackest crime, to matricide, infanticide and fratricide. The deaths are brought about by varying degrees of deliberation, but, though none of these crimes result in legal proceedings, they bring their own nemesis. Each murderous act is committed with the object of changing a situation intolerable to the murderer, and in every case, whether the immediate object is achieved or not, the perpetrator would have done better to have spared the victim. These killings and their detection are, however, not the means of bringing a story to a neat end. Lives continue, relationships are adjusted and personal idiosyncrasies are not transformed by an acquaintance with crime.

The exchange between Sir Godfrey Haslam and his butler Buttermere, with which *Men and Wives* opens has already been quoted. They are joined by Lady Haslam, and Sir Godfrey proceeds to conduct family worship, in which the rather touching muddle of his mental processes is revealed by his extemporary petitions, He prays ' "Keep our daughter, the solace of our age,' " and then, flinching at this hint of senility, modifies the appeal to ' "the companion of her father's prime." ' His prayer that his wife may be sustained through domestic duties gives an only too clear indication that these overwhelm her, after nights that are habitually sleepless. Her tenseness has reached a pitch which causes Anthony Dufferin, the local doctor, to warn Sir Godfrey that additional strain will bring on collapse. The rack on which Harriet Haslam has stretched herself has already been tightened by her disapproval of her children's approach to life. Matthew, qualified as a doctor, ignores his mother's wish that he should practise, and confines himself to research with Dufferin. Jermyn wishes to write creatively rather than to follow an academic career of usefulness. Harriet's intense religious beliefs make her feel that such irresponsibility leads to moral softening in this world and damnation in the next. She is hardly less disapproving of her daughter Griselda's tendency to take too warm an interest in the Reverend Gervase Bellamy. Even her youngest, and favourite, son, Gregory, who endeavours to untangle the knots in his mother's mind, finds her demands are too great. His refuge is in a household of three ageing sisters, and the knowledge that Mrs Calkin, Geraldine Dabis and Kate Dabis have a share in feelings that she thinks should be solely her own is an exacerbation of the grief that possesses Harriet.

The irrational state of Harriet's mind and the pain she inflicts on her family is conveyed with such power that her good qualities are obscured. It is at times difficult to believe that Sir Percy Hardisty, a simple kind man, and Rachel his shrewd and intelligent wife could feel such affection and respect for Harriet as Compton-Burnett would wish her readers to imagine. Rachel Hardisty is, however, prepared to make a remonstrance after Harriet repents an attempt at suicide. Harriet believes she has swallowed a deadly pill, which had been given to her by Doctor Dufferin at her own request.

(Professional standards among medical men in *Men and Wives* are distinctly elastic.)

Rachel tells Harriet's family that their mother can hardly expect not to be the subject of disloyal conversation, after trying to kill herself. ' "I have just been disloyal to her to her face. 'My dear,' I said, when she was afraid she would not sleep. 'It is not your fault that you are not in your last sleep. You do keep changing your mind. It is everything or nothing with you.' " '

The disloyal conversation is interrupted by the reappearance of Sir Godfrey. Earlier in the evening, before the guests arrived for the unexpectedly dramatic dinner-party, Godfrey has displayed himself in a new suit of evening clothes, on which he comments ' "I was meaning to send it back to be altered . . . I suspected a little something across the shoulders, and I was working myself up into a mood. But I don't fancy there is great room for improvement." ' He has, however, been persuaded by his daughter Griselda to change the fancy studs he yearns to wear for some of a plainer pattern. He has returned to the drawing-room to retrieve the more flamboyant studs, which he has concealed behind the clock on the chimney-piece. Having already begun his undressing, he attempts to conceal his gaping shirt-front, but the interest of considering the relative merits of the studs overcomes ideas of modesty. 'Godfrey held the studs before his shirt, waiving compunction in the matter of its expanse. "I don't think they would have done me any good, do you? I think the effect was better without them, just careless enough." '

On the following morning Godfrey has to face the problem of thanking the Almighty for averting Harriet's non-suicide, which he accomplishes by offering thanks for an escape from ' "the great ill, with which Thou wast pleased to threaten us" '. Settling with the Almighty is an easier matter than presenting the neighbours with a story, plausible, but without revealing Harriet's intention. Agatha Calkin and Geraldine Dabis, the more sinister of Gregory Haslam's 'old ladies' make a call of inquiry, but the highly imaginative explanation with which they retreat is a spontaneous offering from Harriet's elder sons.

' "Harriet, I cannot understand why you feel that Matthew and Jermyn should not give themselves to creative work," said Rachel. "Think what they will accomplish in their lives, when they can do so much in few minutes!" '

This relatively gay mood does not endure throughout the day. Harriet becomes more and more unhinged, until Buttermere has the pleasure of asking if arrangements should be made for bringing her ladyship downstairs. Doctor Dufferin's shock treatment appears to have toppled Harriet into collapse. At dinner Godfrey deals with the crisis by an affectionate attempt to feed his wife. Absentmindedly, he then spoons the soup into his own mouth, a sample of the behaviour which has helped to bring Harriet to nervous prostration.

Having announced his intention of visiting his wife every hour throughout the night to observe her condition, Godfrey is obliged to admit, at Matthew's professional interrogation, that he has, himself, slept without waking. Lacking morbidity, Godfrey accepts Harriet's removal to a nursing home with no sense of personal guilt. His children have inherited introspection from their mother, and, in the shock of her illness, resolve to change their ways. Matthew and Jermyn decide to be less self-centred in their ambitions, Griselda and Gregory to shun friendships deprecated by their mother. Rachel Hardisty, who has come to assist the forlorn household, says that she will not take Harriet's place as far as having the room opening out of Godfrey's, but nonetheless she knows how to raise his spirits. At the end of his tether, Godfrey declares that his neighbours have no choice but to reconcile themselves to his low, unwelcoming mood.

' "Yes, so they can," said Rachel. "They soon break the habit of speaking of a friend as an excellent host."
"Why, has anyone ever said that of me?" said Godfrey, sitting up . . .'

The passing of six months shows how well Rachel knows Godfrey's mind, and how shallowly rooted are the resolutions of Harriet's children. Now Matthew has replaced Doctor Dufferin as Camilla's fiancé, and Griselda is engaged to the Reverend Ernest Bellamy (divorced from Camilla) Jermyn's father is to pay for the publication of his son's first book of poems, in addition to buying a house for Matthew and financing Bellamy's theatrical production in aid of the parish church.

Although there are bleatings about economy from Spong, the solicitor, Godfrey has found a great release in a life of worldly pleasure, previously barred to him by the puritanical principles he has shared with his wife. He marvels that he has spent all his life disapproving of the theatre, and, after the performance organised by Bellamy, players and audience are swept back to the Haslam's house. Godfrey has developed his role as 'an excellent host' to the point that his son Matthew, ever a gloomy observer, considers to be foolishly over hospitable. Such entertainments are not to continue. Godfrey's jovial welcome of his neighbours is interrupted by an interview with Doctor Dufferin, which is one of the greatest of Compton-Burnett comic scenes. Dufferin has to break the news to Godfrey that Harriet is now fit to return home, news that it is difficult to persuade the husband to accept. Godfrey fights a rear-guard action with suggestions that Harriet's recovery is more than her family have a right to expect, and that she would be better still left to professional care. Convinced, at last, that there is no escape from this unlooked for boon, Godfrey can only work himself into a proper frame of mind. ' "We take up our old life again, our old life. We go

forward into it, resolute, resigned, rejoicing from our hearts." '
Although the younger children produce a reasonable show of
joy, Matthew, suspecting that Dufferin has manipulated the
situation out of revenge, views Harriet's return as ominous,
and his assessment is correct.

Harriet rejoins her family, in theory only eager to approve
their future plans and their current habits. After an interview with Spong, in which the revelation of Godfrey's spend-
thrift ways is less painful than the evidence that he is at the
mercy of any frivolous influence, Harriet's resolution falters.
Her daemon forces her to return to her old practices of loving
interference. Gregory having repulsed an attempt to wean him
from his habit of visiting Mrs Calkin, Harriet plunges even
deeper, and begs Matthew to delay his marriage. Here she gets
a soothing answer, and a recommendation to take an extra
sleeping-pill, which her eldest son puts ready by her bed.

In the morning, Harriet is found to be, truthfully, in her
last sleep. The coroner is satisfied by evidence that she had
made an opportunity to steal a tablet of fatal properties from
Dufferin's consulting-room. At the funeral, Bellamy gives a
performance judged by himself to be among his best, but
Griselda finds that he needs her to sustain him after this
spending of himself, and has no reserves to comfort her in
her bewilderment at her mother's retreat into a second and
successful suicide. The same bewilderment leads Gregory to
unburden himself to Agatha Calkin, and he, also, feels disillusion, as Mrs Calkin reveals the hollowness of her character
by using the past grief of her widowhood in her attempt to
increase her hold over Gregory. All too soon the Haslams
reach a situation in which they would be glad of the assurance
that Harriet had died by her own hand. Haggard from insomnia, Matthew tells Camilla that he has his mother's death on
his conscience, and begs for her assurance that her love will
surmount this obstacle. Camilla, with some reason, breaks her

engagement in a letter which is a masterpiece of wisdom and self-interest. Her action precipitates Matthew's confession during a breakfast-table drama which, in tension, surpasses any of the many highly strung breakfasts in which Compton-Burnett specialised. Matthew refuses to admit that he is deluded, and that sleep will give him relief, insisting that for one with so little time before him it is not worthwhile to get back into the way of sleeping. Luckily, Dufferin forces Matthew to moderate his position. The doctor points out that, having killed his mother for his own ends and failed in his object, the least he can do is to spare his family further anguish by subscribing to the theory that insomnia, inherited mental instability, and love trouble have brought on this delusion. Buttermere, of course, has overheard everything and accepts the story that Matthew has imagined himself to be a murderer with an increase of professional frigidity of manner. ' "We can hardly expect him not to show his disappointment," said Rachel. "Think of being baulked of what you would like best in the world, when in sight of it!" ' Indeed it is easy to imagine the pleasure with which Buttermere would have taken in inquiring what Sir Godfrey would wish to be done with Mr Matthew's personal effects, immediately after the son's execution by hanging.

Harriet's influence turns out to be far greater after her death than it was in life. Matthew, as has already been mentioned, leaves home for a London practice. Jermyn returns to academic life at Cambridge. Griselda chooses Dufferin, the husband her mother had always wished for her, and Gregory not only publicly casts off his 'old ladies', but marries Polly Hardisty, a girl of his own age. In justice to Mrs Calkin she takes this defection better than her sister Geraldine, who has to struggle for self-control when the youngest sister, Kate, a figure in the background, suddenly becomes engaged to Bellamy.

Harriet's greatest posthumous triumph, however, comes in controlling her husband from beyond the grave. With his family scattered, or about to marry, Godfrey sinks into a lonely reverie, his low-voiced rumblings to himself rising to an angry note as he hears sounds of furtive movements at the door of his library. ' "If that is Buttermere sneaking into the room, he leaves the house this minute!" ' This threat, often invoked by Buttermere's behaviour, is, on this occasion unneeded. It is Camilla who has sneaked into the library, where she finds it an easy matter to arrange for Sir Godfrey to propose to her. He is enchanted with the prospect of a new, fascinating companion and pleasures unknown in his life with Harriet. The vision of love in what Godfrey calls 'the autumn, the later summer of life', evaporates in the course of a business call from Spong. With some circumlocution, Spong breaks it to Godfrey that, by the terms of Harriet's will should he remarry he loses an interest in his first wife's fortune without which he would be unable to live in comfort on his estate. Disbelief is Godfrey's first reaction, followed by depression at the loss of a bright new future. Then his infinite capacity for making the best of things takes over, and soon he is assuring Spong that his wife knew his true heart when she made her constricting will. Spong's own behaviour is guarded, though he hints that he has an appointment with a female friend. Godfrey rejoins his family and the Hardistys at the tea-table. By now he has worked himself into a state of positive exaltation that Harriet prized her husband so highly that she wished to keep him for herself. Any feeling of resentment has been transmuted by Godfrey into a distaste for Spong's attitude, in which he has found symptoms of a belief that Harriet's will has been a shock to her widower. Spong's wife's death, which occurred early in the book, seems to have put him in the same position as Godfrey, the latter feeling it a surprise that one woman could be found to marry Spong, and pooh-poohing the rumour of the solicitor's engagement. Buttermere gets in a final jab by confirming this rumour while he is shaking out the tea-cloth. Guesses are made as to whom Spong is engaged, Godfrey, rather viciously guessing Mrs Calkin. In fact, Godfrey has to face the news that Spong is engaged to Camilla. After expressing disbelief, and disgust at such a girl marrying a man nearly as old as he is himself, Godfrey finds yet again a consoling thought. Camilla, he suggests, will bring no more people to grief. He can even express amusement (which he changes to 'satisfaction') that Harriet has tied up the loose ends of her family's life exactly as she wished, ' "Harriet was always a fortunate woman," said Rachel.'

If there is a villain in *Men and Wives*, it is not the agonised Matthew, matricide though he be. It is Dominic Spong who is most qualified for the role, his sententiousness having a sinister undercurrent that brings to mind another solicitor-clown, Widmerpool in Anthony Powell's *A Dance to the Music of Time*. On the day of his first wife's funeral Spong accepts a round of social engagements, ending with a call on Doctor Dufferin. There he has a voyeur's treat, for Camilla arrives and, being at that moment engaged to Dufferin, seats herself on her fiancé's knee. From then, until he finally captures her, Spong uses all his tenacity to bring about a situation in which Camilla will see him as the most advantageous match at her disposal. Sir Godfrey remarked that at least this marriage will inhibit Camilla's power for mischief, but the reader may have some doubts that, should a richer, more glamorous *parti* appear, Camilla would be shown to have kept her matrimonial volatility. Spong may be the villain, but Sir Godfrey is the hero of *Men and Wives*. He is the first of a row of baronets, the most guileless and the most charming. His vanity is transparent, and so is his anger—' "Buttermere, sound that gong in the proper manner . . . or leave the house." ' Rachel

33

Hardisty compares with Godfrey as the queen in chess compares with the king, dealing with his blunders with a tenderness that is lacking in her commerce with other neighbours. Rachel is rare among Compton-Burnett women of strong character in that she does not abuse her power, and also that she is not incapable of self-criticism.

6

A SCHOOL AND ITS RULER

The qualities of controlling her own power and of criticising her own behaviour do not belong to Josephine Napier, the principal character in *More Women than Men*, Compton-Burnett's most successful school story. It is a school story of much originality in that its concern is almost solely with the staff. In *Pastors and Masters* the pupils have been described as a frieze of hobgoblins in the background. At Josephine Napier's school the pupils are so far in the background as to be practically invisible. The book opens with Mrs Napier interviewing her staff at the beginning of a new term. Created by herself, the school gives her a platform from which she directs her world to move as she wishes, inhaling at the same time the incense of flattery offered to her by the more uncritical of her dependants. Consequently, her separate welcomes to her staff are like a sequence of tiny ballets, in each of which the prima ballerina adjusts her mood to her momentary partner in a *pas de deux*.

For Miss Luke there is a simple, kind, domestic welcome, but with the inscrutable Miss Rosetti a more cautious approach is necessary. As the plot develops so does the emotional rapport between the two women, but at the moment Josephine rejects Miss Rosetti's suggestion that she might buy a partnership in the school. In spite of their verbal fencing, it is clear from the first that Miss Rosetti sees the headmistress without illusion.

35

' "You are very kind," Mrs Napier.
"No. Why am I kind?" said Josephine, seeming to speak in
an aside from jotting something down. "You have always done
all you can for me."
"I will certainly do it, Mrs Napier," said Miss Rosetti, her
eyes just resting on Josephine's empty page, as she left the
room.'

With her own knowledge of Josephine to use for her own
purposes, Miss Rosetti is, at the same time, prepared to keep
in step with her employer. Miss Munday, the senior mistress,
has an equal perception of Josephine's character, but makes no
effort to compromise, finding it difficult to keep a serious face
when Josephine fishes in vain for a statement that the term is
better and more satisfying than the holidays. Like a good
poker player, Miss Munday is chary of her words, and she is
also qualified by a degree to teach English to the senior forms.
The more lowly branches of English literature are taught by
Mrs Chattaway, an unkempt little fieldmouse of a widow, her
qualification being that her husband wrote. Towards her Mrs
Napier can be as unrestrained as she wishes, in the assurance
that she will only receive unfeigned admiring gratitude from
Mrs Chattaway, though even here there has to be a kind but
firm squashing of the idea that to work for bread is fundamen-
tally a mortification. Finally, Josephine has to greet a talented
newcomer, Helen Keats, who she despatches to the senior
common-room with maternal urgings to make a good tea and
fatten up her pale slenderness. In the common-room emotions
other than maternal are apparent, Miss Keats' charms are not
considered to need improvement, and in the spate of feminine
feelings Mrs Chattaway is rudderless. Remarking to Miss
Munday on the devotion between Miss Luke and Miss Rosetti
she gets a reply which indicates, to the reader if not to Mrs
Chattaway, that Miss Munday has passed through an emotional relationship with both these fellow-teachers. Upstairs,

Miss Luke cannot refrain from commenting that Miss Rosetti
has cast a warm eye on Miss Keats, which Miss Rosetti does
not deny. Nor does she contradict another theory, subsequently confirmed by events, and now put forward by Miss
Luke, that Miss Rosetti is also cherishing an unconscious passion for their headmistress. In the meantime, Miss Rosetti
cherishes Miss Keats in a practical manner by offering to
bring the young girl's wardrobe up to date.

Another homosexual relation is working itself towards a
change in the house of Josephine Napier's brother, Jonathan
Swift, so christened by their parents in the hope that a great
man's name would bring greatness with it. This hope unreal-
ised, Jonathan has eked out an unedifying career in Holy
Orders by the help of pupils. In the case of Felix Bacon the
pupilage has lasted for twenty-two years as a contented love-
affair. That is to say Jonathan and Felix have been contented,
but a heavy cloud of disapproval emanates from Felix's home,
where his father, a widowed baronet distrusts, not without
reason, a situation that appears to him unnatural. Felix's
sprightliness is undiminished by twenty-two years under
Jonathan's roof, but the latter is conscious that Felix's eye is
beginning to rove. Jonathan is even made nervous by Felix's
interest in Gabriel, Jonathan's son who has been adopted and
brought up by Josephine and her husband, Simon Napier.
Gabriel has, already, a heavy emotional burden to bear, for
Josephine's affection is now wholly directed towards her
adopted son, leaving her husband in an unenviably subordi-
nate position, both in his home and in his wife's school.

Josephine and her family dine with Jonathan, Felix and
Jonathan's other lodger, a solicitor called Fane, who almost
equals Dominic Spong in crassness. Fane has also a strong
curiosity on most matters though he does not direct it towards
the relationship of his landlord with his fellow lodger. Instead
he presses his inquiries into Josephine's rise to her present suc-

cessful position, and in the course of the evening's talk Felix incites Josephine to engage him as a drawing-master. (It is at this point that he makes the rather anachronistic telephone call to his father.) Josephine is definitely excited by the prospect of employing Felix, and deals briskly with Fane's inquiry if she did not object to a male teacher in her school.

' "No," said Josephine, "I do not see any reason for objecting to it. With certain things granted, of course."

"They are all granted with me," said Felix. "I do not even like to have such things talked about." '

The excitements of the evening are not over. On returning to the headmistress's house a figure from the past meets Josephine and Simon. Elizabeth Giffard, a widow with an only daughter, has sought them out in an appeal for help, after twenty years of struggling to bring up her child. In the course of the reunion it becomes clear that Simon was in love with Elizabeth at the time of her marriage, and that Josephine suppressed the news of Elizabeth's early widowhood until she had safely accomplished her own marriage to Simon. Josephine is made too toughly to be embarrassed at her manoeuvre becoming known to her husband and his former love, and the revelation does not hinder her from offering Elizabeth a post as housekeeper, with employment also for Ruth, her daughter.

Tragedy upon tragedy follows this act of magnanimity, beginning with a disaster at the school prize-giving. Felix's father, Sir Robert Bacon, appears at this function, and though, not unnaturally, Jonathan slinks away, Felix himself is undaunted in his whimsical promotion of his position of drawing-master. This enthusiasm leads to a confrontation between Elizabeth and Josephine, the latter sending the former to search for a portfolio illustrating the work of Felix's pupils, and the former, in rebellion at Josephine's high-handed authority, publicly annexing Simon to help her. From the top of the library ladder, Simon makes something approaching a declaration of renewed love to Elizabeth, but she, startled by the sound of Josephine's step, lets go her hold of the ladder and brings Simon down in a fall which mortally injures him. Although she has overheard Simon's words of love to Elizabeth, Josephine swims effortlessly into the part of the inconsolable survivor of a marriage of perfect happiness, ordering widow's weeds of an exaggerated sombreness considered old-fashioned by the standards of the day. She is still adding touches to this new rôle, though her performance in the mistresses' common-room has already a fine polish, when Josephine is attacked by a revolt within her family. Gabriel and Ruth, the daughter of Elizabeth Giffard, announce they wish to be married. The resultant battle ends with a temporary set-back for Josephine in that the marriage does take place, assisted by an anonymously given allowance, which is presumed to come from Jonathan. Josephine can only emphasise her feelings by appearing at the wedding in her ostentatiously black widow's garb, but she has a sympathiser in Felix, who suggests that disillusion with Gabriel and jealousy of his feeling for Ruth will, inevitably, leave the survivors of the family group to become more to each other.

When this process is interrupted by the return of the young couple, it is at once clear that Ruth, although suffering from incipient pneumonia, is determined to battle with Josephine, whose hold on Gabriel has not been loosened by his marriage. Moved by the struggle of the sick girl, Josephine persuades Gabriel that his absence will relieve the jealous strain, so that when the illness reaches its crisis she, alone, is in charge of Ruth. In her delirium the girl tries to rise from her bed, and Josephine, for a moment, succumbs to the temptation to expose Ruth to an icy draught, in a manner that may prevent her recovery and so remove this obstacle that has come between Gabriel and his adopted mother. The draught has been made colder by the entrance of Miss Rosetti, who accepts

Josephine's explanation—that Ruth was too strong to be restrained—with a certain reserve in her manner, and a sceptical glance at her headmistress's powerful figure.

Whether from this exposure, or by the normal course of her illness, Ruth dies, leaving Josephine, once again, in possession of Gabriel. Josephine's first step is to offer Miss Rosetti, sole witness of her murderous impulse, the partnership she had previously refused to the younger mistress. Accepting the implication that this is a bribe, Miss Rosetti herself now refuses the offer, because, she says, enigmatically, she is no longer in a position to buy her share of the partnership. The question of a financial share in the school had a considerable fascination for I. Compton-Burnett. Looking back to *Pastors and Masters*, it will be recalled that Mr Merry's concern that the reckless use of coal should not eat up the profits of the school opens the book. In a later book, *Two Worlds and Their Ways* there is a wonderful exchange on the subject of withdrawal of pupils without adequate notice, and finally, in *The Last and the First*, to buy a partnership in a school represents an act of liberation for a frustrated unmarried daughter.

It has been pointed out earlier that death dealers in Compton-Burnett plots are apt to defeat their own ends. Josephine is faced by a sudden change in herself. Finding that possession of Gabriel no longer satisfies her, she realizes that he has been replaced in her affections by Felix. For her Felix's gay prophecy that they would become more to each other has been proved to be true. Never lacking in decision, Josephine corrals Miss Keats as someone who may console Gabriel, temporarily or even permanently. There is a need to act quickly as Sir Robert, father of Felix, is moving towards his death-bed. The prospect of Felix leaving the school to enjoy his inheritance incites Josephine to get to work on a new verbal self-portrait, a representation of someone young for

her age, who is preparing to free herself more frequently
from the burden of the school. This change of tune leads to
her referring to herself as Gabriel's 'aunt-sister', where
previously she has wavered between an adopted mother and
any woman in relation to any man.

The death of Felix's father makes it clear that Felix will
be leaving Jonathan as well as the school. It is while attempting to plan a new life for her brother that Josephine discovers
that Gabriel's mother is Miss Rosetti, and that the money set
aside for the purchase of the partnership has made up the
anonymous allowance for which Jonathan has had the credit.
Josephine breaks out in protest at the deceit that has been
practised on her by Gabriel's father and mother, but
Jonathan, seated at his desk refuses to accept that his sister
has a cause of complaint. '[Jonathan] moved his fingers as
though he were playing the piano, and moved his lips as if
in song.' Later, he moves his hands and feet together, 'adding
the pedals to his performance'. As he is losing Felix, Jonathan
cares little as to how the situation will sort itself out. Felix
has, of course, always known the truth about Gabriel's
parentage, but now he learns that Jonathan has taken the
credit that belongs to Gabriel's mother for their son's support.
The knowledge adds a gloss of cheerfulness to their imminent
parting. ' "I always wondered how you got the money. I
like to think I have been the intimate of a bad man." . . .
Felix locked his arm in Jonathan's and danced across the
room. The old man fell out in a moment, stiff and breathless.
' "Ah, there is a parable! I have gone far enough at your
side. I can go no further." '

Josephine faces Miss Rosetti in a show-down in which the
headmistress is buoyed up by the expectation of an interview
with Felix. As Miss Rosetti points out neither Josephine nor
herself is in a position to reveal the whole of their past
histories, and this leads Miss Rosetti to explain that she has

not cared for Gabriel. She has, she says, cared for the women for whom she has wished to care, and the woman she has come, almost involuntarily, to care for most is Josephine herself. The mysterious allowance to Gabriel is now transformed into Miss Rosetti's contribution for a partnership in the school, but, although Josephine has accepted her new partner's declaration of love without surprise, she is still expecting a heterosexual declaration from Felix. Her announcement of her new partnership, with a hint that this may leave her free for other commitments, brings a blow in the face from Felix, who announces his engagement to Helen Keats. Maria Rosetti shows the strength of her admiration for Josephine's fortitude by taking over the inquiries natural to the moment. Left alone with Josephine, it is a sympathetic word from Maria that causes the pair 'to fall into their first embrace'.

The wedding visit to Sir Felix and Lady Bacon is paid by Josephine, Jonathan and Gabriel, the family party being augmented by William Fane. It would have been better had Fane been left at home, for, in a cross-purpose conversation with Gabriel, he makes it clear that Miss Rosetti is responsible for the allowance whose provenance has varied between Jonathan and Josephine. Gabriel is forced into maturity by the consequent revelations, which give him more of a jolt than the death of his bride. He baulks at the prospect of living in the same house as his father, his real mother, his adopted mother and his mother-in-law. Escaping from this plethora of parents, he arranges to remove his father and to live with him in a house managed by Elizabeth, his mother-in-law. This setting up of what might be called a colony of losers, leaves the winners in possession of the school. In an interview between the mother and son the lack of sympathy is such that, Miss Rosetti is justified in remarking to Josephine than she will never again speak as a mother.

Josephine pays a final visit to the mistresses' common-room. Once again she turns to building herself up as All-Wise in her dealings. She explains that to bring Gabriel to understand that it is his duty to make a home for his father has been an obligation she has long laboured to fulfill. There are reasons, she says that would make Jonathan's residence in her house unsuitable.

' "My brother is, if you will not misunderstand me, very much of a man."

"We will not misunderstand you," said Miss Munday.'

Miss Luke hurriedly changes the conversation to the Bacons' new home, but this leads to another pitfall. Mrs Chattaway blurts out that someone, foolishly, had once said that Felix and Josephine had wanted to marry. Josephine deals with this turning of a worm by expressing surprise at the repetition of such an idle rumour, leaving the common-room with the castle of her self-esteem repaired. With a display of gusto, she refuses Miss Rosetti's offer to interview an applicant for the post of drawing-master. Indeed her references to her state of widowhood and her sombre figure show more sexual consciousness than may be agreeable to her new partner. As Josephine makes her last exit to do her best with this ' "male aspirant to my post" ', the reader can understand why Felix and Helen felt home-sick and out of things when they had left the dramas of the school for their sedate country-house life.

With the solitary exception of the disapproving Sir Robert Bacon, none of the inverted relationships of *More Women than Men*, are treated with surprise by any of the onlookers. The convention is observed that Gabriel's illegitimate birth should be concealed by a fable that Jonathan's non-existent wife had died, but abnormality is scarcely disguised and is no handicap to the success of the school. Incidentally, although this establishment is the means of livelihood of the principal characters, it is seen entirely from the managerial point of view. The educational process and the pupils exposed to it remain undescribed, except on the occasion of the school concert when playing the violin, presenting a bouquet to the headmistress and dropping a tray of tea-cups is the extent of the girls' activities. The parents of the pupils are poor in spirit, lacking the lively bad-temper of Mr Bentley (*Pastors and Masters*) which led to his strictures on the instructor of his sons. Accepting that Josephine floats on a level above that inhabited by the girls in her care, a mother humbly asks Josephine if someone can write to her about her daughter's violin tuition.

' "I *hope* to write to you myself," said Josephine, emphasising her second word, and leaving [the mother] in favour of the state it indicated, as compared with certainty.' With passions among the staff swinging loose like power belts slipped from their rollers, the girls of Josephine's school may be considered fortunate that their headmistress claims only to know them by sight.

7

TYRANNY BREEDS
CONTEMPT

'[King Louis XIV said furiously] "Thank God she [la duchesse de Bourgogne, wife of his heir] has miscarried since it was bound to happen! Now, perhaps, I shall not be thwarted in my excursions and everything else that I want to do, by doctors' orders and midwives argufying. At last, I can come and go as I please and they will leave me in peace." A silence during which you might have heard an ant walking succeeded this outburst . . . Stupefaction reigned. Even the gardeners stood still. The silence lasted for fully a quarter of an hour.

'It was the King himself who broke it by leaning over the balustrade and speaking of a carp. No one answered him. Thereafter, he addressed his remarks about carp to the gardeners, who were not usually included in his conversation . . . It was all vastly dull and the King went away soon afterwards.'

Louis XIV at Marly. Memoirs of Saint-Simon, 1708.

The genius of Saint-Simon has here described a scene of unmitigated selfishness which still shouts from the page. Surrounded by parasites, who depended on him for everything that made their life worth living, Louis XIV found that he had passed the point when his behaviour was uncriticised, if only by silent stupefaction. He found that even a return to

45

graciousness could not restore the respectful adulation which had rendered his morning walk in the gardens so agreeable.

If this piece of historical reporting is compared with Compton-Burnett's portraits of male and female domestic tyrants it will be seen how penetrating was her comprehension of the psychology of despotism. Nowhere is this more striking than in A House and Its Head, a book which is not only one of the highest peaks in the mountain range of Compton-Burnett's literary achievement, but a book in which the head of the house is peculiarly extravagant in his display of tyranny. Duncan Edgeworth's insistence on absolute power over his family brings a nemesis both violent and subtle, but he has an ability to talk his way out of the most shameful predicaments, a gift Louis XIV might well have envied.

As has been mentioned earlier, A House and Its Head opens on Christmas Day in the year 1885. Duncan, described as young for his sixty-six years, and his wife Ellen are waiting for the belated appearance at the breakfast table of Nance and Sybil, their daughters, and of Grant, Duncan's nephew and heir. Ellen, who has a 'harried, innocent, somehow fulfilled expression', is about sixty, and, as her daughter Sybil is only eighteen, Ellen would appear to be an example of Compton-Burnett's practice of making mothers of what might more usually be grandmothers. This situation occurs again later in the novel, the author, on the whole, not considering that a decline in fertility might take place after age of forty.

Duncan's victimisation of his wife takes the form of parsimony in domestic matters, and lack of consideration for her deteriorating health. Nance is her mother's unsuccessful protector, but Sybil, a natural double dealer, fawns on her father, as the figure of power, and despises her mother for her submission to his callousness. After the Christmas greetings, exchanges used by Duncan as an opportunity to inquire into his family's religious attitudes, Grant is observed by his uncle to have received, as a gift from Ellen, a book described as 'a scientific work inimical to the faith of the day'. Ignoring that Ellen must have spent money she cannot afford on this present, Duncan at once places it on the fire, fuel not being, apparently, among his economies.

' "Have you read the book, Father?" [said Nance] "From cover to cover. And on every page there is poison. My volume met the fate of this one." '

A trifle anachronistically, Grant remarks that the function of this pernicious volume does seem to be to keep the home fires burning. Contretemps follows contretemps. Hardly has the unhappy Ellen brought herself to confess that she has had no surplus from the Christmas expenses to buy presents for the household staff, than Grant's morals come up for censure. He has been observed in making all too public advances to a maidservant. Duncan's reproof is tempered by his respect for Grant as a male and his pleasure in his nephew's company. This attachment is so deeply imbedded in Duncan's nature that it even survives the bitterness of later sufferings. Grant's opportunist habit of seduction, combined with an incriminating lock of white hair inherited from his own mother's side of the family and passed on to Duncan's supposed son, wrecks Duncan's second marriage.

Although the minor characters of Compton-Burnett novels are sometimes condemned to have no redeeming feature, this is not generally true of the major characters. A moment of pathos or magnanimity can make even the victims of the villains and villainesses say a word in their oppressors's favour, while a relapse into dishonesty or unkindness often causes the more attractive characters to lose their appeal. Nance Edgeworth is the exception. As the merciless searchlight plays over the enclosed world of the Edgeworth family illuminating oppression of the helpless, cupidity prepared to instigate murder, and amours based on the crudest sexual gratification, Nance stands out, isolated in her goodness. This saved soul in the company of the damned is as near a heroine as the author ever allowed herself to create.

Having squashed a futile attempt by Grant at rebelling, Duncan leads his family to church, and afterwards into the churchyard which is where the social analysis of the neighbourhood is carried out by the gentlefolk of the parish. Oscar Jekyll, the rector, conducts the service in a manner so restrained that a parishoner has remarked 'that faith as deep as his could hardly appear on the surface'. Actually, the surface is where Oscar's faith exists, but he considers that his adequate performance of his duties permits him to continue in the church, as he has to support Gretchen, his widowed mother. Six small boy pupils contribute to Oscar's income, but his sister Cassandra is not a burden. She has been governess to Sybil and Nance, and has continued to live in their father's house. It is an arrangement advantageous to the family as she can ride out the storms of Duncan's temper more equably than his immediate kindred. Consequently she enjoys an equality of friendship denied to most of the instructresses in Compton-Burnett schoolrooms.

Besides the Jekylls, three other families assemble in the churchyard. Doctor and Mrs Smollett are a worldly-wise couple, in contrast to Miss Rosamund Burtenshaw and her cousin Beatrice Fellowes. This pair live with Alexander, father of Rosamund, who exists philosophically with a daughter who only ceased to be a missionary because of the discomfort of the life, and a niece who performs spiritual good works at the slightest opportunity. Mr and Mrs Bode, their son Almeric and their daughter Dulcia complete the local circle. Almeric, although he plays a vital part in the drama of the Edgeworth's lives, is not described in depth, his main characteristics being literary aspirations which have only led him to 'honest despair of contemporary work' and a wincing distaste for the goings-on of his sister Dulcia. This slangy hoyden is blithely uncaring of her brother's feelings, and forges ahead on a course which starts with patronising bullying of her parents, and arrives, by way of gossip, at spreading cruellest slander. She is not the wickedest of Compton-Burnett hoydens, a position pre-empted by Anna Donne in *Elders and Betters*, but her heavy-handed interventions invariably worsen painful situations. There are hints of these troubles to come in Sybil's self-conscious efforts to attract male attention by catching her hair in a bush, in Florence Smollett's shrewd awareness that Ellen's health is threatened, and in rivalry for the rector's notice from those co-workers for the church, Miss Burtenshaw and Miss Fellowes.

The afternoon of Christmas is enlivened by Grant's take-off of Oscar Jekyll's sermon. Cassandra Jekyll has explained that her brother fancies that his congregation like exposition rather than reproach, and Grant follows this idea, ' ". . . To draw a line between the brain and what is called the soul, is to break up the entity that is the self of each, into parts that are inorganic and meaningless—" ' This performance takes place in the schoolroom, a social womb to which Duncan banishes the younger generation, only to forbid them its refuge at a change of mood. Such bursts of laughter come from the audience, augmented by Almeric and Dulcia Bode, that Bethia the parlourmaid is sent to complain of the noise. Never one to allow herself to be worsted in repartee, Bethia is knocking the conversational bowling to the boundary when Duncan appears to protest in person. Duncan accepts the shuffling excuse by Grant that he was impersonating ' "any clergyman" ', merely accusing his nephew of besmirching the cloth and belated boyishness.

' "Uncle is a weak character," said Grant.

"No, he is simple and strong," said Almeric.'

These opposing points of view are developed later in the book, when both speakers inflict the same injury, wife-stealing, on Duncan. Comprehending his own kin, Grant stands firm in circumstances of considerable stress, while Almeric, a stranger, takes the opportunity of escaping from a neighbourhood in which Duncan is at the apex of local society. Almeric is a rarity in Compton-Burnett novels by the completeness of his success in escaping to an existence of ordinary domesticity.

Christmas Day draws to a weary close, with Ellen almost too exhausted to face the turkey, even though Duncan has recovered his temper at the sight of this noble bird. His temper needed recovering as it had been ruffled by a call from Beatrice Fellowes, on a supererogatory round of visits to repeat the message of Christmas once again to her neighbours. Their reactions are, on the whole, discouraging, Mrs Jekyll, for example, asking the unanswerable question as to why she thinks they have not received the Christmas message as much as herself.

'Ellen took a hand of each of her daughters, and spoke and wept at the same time.'

' "... I must stay at home to-day ... I have been ill less often than I ought in my life, because Father hated illness. I must sometimes be like other people. This house has to be so different from other houses; and lately I have felt it is too much for me, all this difference." ' This collapse of Ellen's has come at a Sunday breakfast, of which Nance says she images a climax of disagreeableness has been attained. Although warned that Ellen is not well, Duncan obliges her, by the force of years of accumulated bullying, to come down to breakfast. On the way to church he continues to beat off attempts to confront him with reality, deftly turning Sybil and Grant's anxiety into a 'show' brought on by their feeling a need for drama in their smooth and easy life. He even goes as far as to display doubts of Doctor Smollett's capabilities. It would be better, he is heard to say, if Ellen was about among them and then, if they thought it needful, proper medical advice, source unspecified, could be sought. Even though Smollett is sent for during the service, Duncan continues to fight a rear-guard action among his kindly inquiring friends in the churchyard. He puts forward the view, rightly called very odd by Grant, that the general feeling that there is not much amiss is a good touchstone.

'Helpless in the grip of the morning's mood', it is not until Ellen is seen to be dying that Duncan shows any sympathy for his wife, as she lies worrying over unpaid bills about which she has not had the courage to approach him. At her last breath, Ellen says she knows that Nance has loved her and with her last gasp she gives a cry from the heart as to how much better Cassie and Grant make things for us, an 'us' that her family know is in opposition to Duncan's 'I'.

Ellen's death leaves Duncan without the most vulnerable of his domestic targets, but only reluctantly does he allow grief and remorse to drive out his devil of self-righteousness. Ellen, he says, was fortunate in not having to keep up and about on the last Sunday of her life, and in being protected by her husband's prescience from the harassment of exaggerated concern. He is only driven from the table when Nance finds the costly arrangements for her mother's funeral too painful a contrast with the stringency of Ellen's daily life to be passed over in silence.

The funeral ceremony gives an opening for Beatrice Fellowes to assure Oscar that the family will have appreciated his address, though they could, of course, give no outward sign. As Oscar remarks aside to his mother, Ellen's family could hardly have wished for the occasion to arise and so he had not looked for applause. Dulcia piles on more embarrassment by taking it upon herself to thank Doctor Smollett for his care of Mrs Edgeworth and then getting in a tangle about the fatal outcome of the illness. However, Dulcia manages to see the occasion as what she calls a red-letter day by having her request granted to call Miss Fellowes by her christian name of Beatrice. This is a score for Beatrice in her perpetual rivalry with her cousin, but Rosamund manages to even the score by representing Dulcia's advance as something her own qualities of age and dignity would necessarily preclude.

At the Edgeworths' house Duncan relieves feelings he has suppressed at the funeral by wailings of almost animal intensity at his inability ever to have shown Ellen how much he loved her. Nance has pity on her father's pain at facing past miseries of which he has been the instrument, and her reassuring words, that she knew Ellen had loved her husband for what he was, leads to an hour's session with Duncan in his library. Nance reports to the rest of the family.

' "I feel I have lost both my parents. Mother has not vanished more completely than Father. In his stead there is a man, who has been an almost monotonously amiable husband . . ." '
Nance adds that it is fortunate that she is not a person who cannot tell a lie. She has practically forgotten the difference between truth and falsehood, which has ceased to be of any concern of Duncan's. This patching of Duncan's ego is shared, and indeed almost taken over, by Sybil. Duncan's dependence on her, she finds to be a reward for the nervous strain, but she pays a sinister penalty in the increase of her obsession with her father and with the importance of the family inheritance. Only Grant remains aloof from administering the injections of fantasy to which Duncan has become addicted. This restraint gains respect from his uncle. 'To Duncan those who rendered service existed to serve.'

Among Duncan's gestures of mourning is the rehanging of Ellen's portrait in the dining-room, though he is dissatisfied by his family's rather temperate reaction. To Sybil's inquiry if he had, himself, transferred the picture, Duncan asks if he would have allowed any hand but his to touch it.

' "I thought I saw some plaster on the landing," said Nance.' Suddenly there is a promise of a respite from Duncan's demands. Aunt Maria, his widowed invalid sister has, he tells the company, invited him to pay her a visit. Stunned at the prospect of even a brief spell of liberty, Duncan's family wobble between urging him on and trying to conceal their anxiety for his departure. The departure itself is only achieved after a prolonged game of cat and mouse by Duncan, including an agonising return after he has once driven from the house. As Grant says, only his uncle's death could resolve the situation, and when the traveller has truly gone the chapter ends with an almost audible sigh of relief.

The shadow that Duncan's return, although delayed, will finally take place, and that Ellen will come no more, hangs over the parentless household and inhibits any exuberance. Finally, urged by Dulcia as a duty to Ellen's friends, there is an informal party, at which Sybil continues her unpromising pursuit of Almeric. This pursuit is interrupted by sounds of an unexpected arrival, but hopes for the excitement of a stranger in this enclosed world are blighted by Bethia's throwaway remark that it is only the master. The appropriate quotation is supplied by the elder and most quick-witted of Duncan's daughters.

' "My father is come!" quoted Nance, "He is in the hall at this moment." '

Duncan finds the mice playing innocuously, compared with the antics Sir Thomas Bertram broke up by his unheralded return to Mansfield Park. It is, on this occasion, the home-comer who provides the sensation. Duncan shatters the composure of the gathering by announcing his approaching marriage. From the experience of her long life, Mrs Jekyll offers the consolation of normality to the silenced company.

' "You can't any of you know what a usual thing this is," said Gertrude in a comfortable tone.'

Having learnt from their father that their prospective step-mother is young and beautiful, his daughters are faced with the question as to what should be done about Ellen's portrait, and Sybil goes so far as to appeal to her father not to bring an interloper to sit beneath it. Brushed aside by Duncan, Sybil then appeals to the others to agree that the newcomer cannot possibly be nice. Although his position as heir is being threatened, Grant is prepared to be generous. He points out that anyone taking on Duncan as a husband must be brave, hopeful and very affectionate to have become fond of his uncle, which, combined with youth and beauty, would make up a character of extreme niceness. This partiality of Grant's is only too prophetic. Alison, the second Mrs Edgeworth, is all that her bridegroom has described, and Grant's infatuation is immediately apparent.

The drama of Duncan's second marriage develops swiftly and inexorably. Alison finds her situation as the wife of a well-established domestic tyrant uncongenial, being by age and temperament on the side of the oppressed. By the social moot in the churchyard, she is accepted with enthusiasm, Dulcia giving an officious assurance that all prejudice has faded before Alison's charm. Almeric's feelings are even stronger, while Alison's first victim, Grant, shaken out of his coolness remarks to Nance that Dulcia has ' "no right to live" '.

Breakers are ahead, as Mrs Jekyll says, and the storm rises at luncheon. Duncan's gloom at Alison's references to his first marriage, and to the removal, by Grant, of Ellen's portrait drives Alison from the room. Grant takes the opportunity of making her a declaration, which she takes lightly. In the evening, an affectionate scene between Duncan and Alison is observed by Grant, of whose presence Alison is aware.

Duncan, 'tired by the subtle demand of the day' goes to bed, leaving Alison sexually wrought up, and Grant prepared to make the most of his opportunity.

Nine months later Dulcia runs boisterously from house to house announcing the birth of a son to Alison. She gaily admits her foolishness in breaking the news to the Smolletts, the doctor having presided at the birth, and moves on to the refrain of rejoicing with the Edgeworths because a son has been born unto them. Her circuit recalls Beatrice Fellowes' Christmas expedition to reinforce the message of Christ's birth, and she gets an equally grim response from Gertrude Jekyll, who remarks that Grant's nose is now out of joint.

At the christening party for the infant Richard the neighbourhood can watch, in excitement barely tempered with regret, the jangling of tempers between Duncan and Alison, the free use of her christian name which she permits to her neighbours, rankling particularly with her husband. Never without spirit, Alison points out that Almeric Bode, and the other guests, have been in the habit of saying 'Mrs Edgeworth' to someone else. Almeric's attentions to Alison are a matter of complaint from Sybil to Dulcia, and her suspicions are prophetic, for Alison is not long to retain the position for whose dignities she has such a carefree disregard.

As he is about to leave the house for some days, Duncan becomes aware that Marshall, nurse of the infant Richard is being dismissed. The reason, that Marshall is yet another victim of Grant's penchant for seducing maidservants, is put forward by Cassie with less than her usual poise. Shortly afterwards smouldering animosities break out into a blaze of revealed scandal. Duncan, still absent, sends Alison a note enclosing a letter from Marshall, the dismissed nurse, to say that little Richard has a white streak in his hair, showing that Grant is his real father. Cassie and Nance are already in the secret, and now they find it necessary to explain matters to

Sybil, though Cassie checks morbid inquiries as to when the conception took place. As Cassie says, it is best to let anyone in a great difficulty get out of it in any way that comes to mind. For Alison the way is provided by Almeric, who comes to call and with whom she is seen to be walking down the drive and out of the story.

The rest cannot flee from Duncan's wrath to come. Although Nance says that tragedy truly inspires terror and pity and that in her terror is getting the upper hand, by the time of Duncan's arrival emotion is exhausted. Only Sybil, the ambiguity of whose behaviour is not yet fully revealed, casts herself upon her father and begs him to send to the Bode's house, where, she says, Alison might be found waiting for her husband's forgiveness. Even Compton-Burnett does not attempt to paint the scene at the Bodes' house, where Duncan at once makes a far from ordinary social call. On his return he confirms that Alison and Almeric have fled together, and forbids any mention of their names, ' "at this time, at a future time, at any time in our lives, or in your lives after mine" '.

The optimism of this ruling is shown to be ill-founded, as the parents and sister of Almeric arrive to call early on the following morning. Mrs Bode's weeping is interrupted by the wish that she had never been a mother, but Dulcia, now unrestrained by Almeric, strikes more extreme attitudes, accepting Duncan's announcing that he will divorce Alison as just and wise.

' "To think that Dulcia is not the child Mrs Bode is weeping for!" murmured Nance.'

Grant's return to an interview with his uncle is the next ordeal. Gradually, after a moment of violence when he strikes Grant in the face, Duncan talks himself into a state when he is able to point out that Grant's punishment for fathering Richard is his own disinheritance. Grant can even feel that a warning not to carry his habit of seduction among his cousins, conceals, in spite of his behaviour, an intimation that he will be accepted as a son-in-law.

Consequently, Grant celebrates the divorce of Duncan from Alison by proposing to Nance. It is surprising, he points out, considering how much has come to light, that he would have no secrets from her. Nance is firmly against the idea of marrying her cousin, on the excellent grounds that she feels to him as a sister, and that there is somebody else. Their next step is to discuss the advisability of Grant marrying Sybil. He points out the Sybil cannot expect his heart at her feet as hers is ' "not at disposal at all. It is odd that she and Alison both prefer Almeric to me" '. Grant assures Sybil that she makes him very happy, by accepting his proposal and saving him from the contempt of Duncan who always seems to have been accepted. This axiom turns out, once again, to be true, for, having welcomed Grant as a son, Duncan proposes to Cassie who is prepared to become the third Mrs Edgeworth. She is, says Nance, the one woman whose marriage to Duncan will allow Ellen's portrait to remain in the dining-room. While their relationship is still unaltered, Nance takes the opportunity to ask Cassie why she wants to marry Nance's father. With stark realism, Cassie replies that, as she has lived under Duncan's roof for twenty years, it is unremarkable that she can face the prospect of an assured future in his company.

At the wedding of Grant and Sybil, a close observer will remark that there are exchanges between Oscar Jekyll and Nance which indicate why she refused Grant's proposal. (Indeed, unless Nance had lost her heart to the egregious Mr Burtenshaw there is no other unmarried man available.) In an aside Dulcia mentions that Alison and Almeric are prospering, but that it will be impossible for them to visit Almeric's parents during Duncan's lifetime, rejecting Nance's suggestion that they could be alerted if Duncan was going away, to save the tedium of waiting for his death.

From her honeymoon, Sybil sends the news that she is expecting a child, and also that she has lost her diamond brooch, a wedding present from Duncan. Her father makes sardonic comments on both these pieces of news. He feels impatience at the carelessness over the brooch, and, as Cassie is expecting a child herself, he is scornful of Sybil's importance over her own prospects. He has also a complaint as to the noisiness of Richard, 'the brat' upstairs. But now horror creeps into the story. Richard, child of the brief liaison between Alison and Grant, is found dead in his gas-filled nursery, apparently the victim of his own curiosity in fiddling with gas taps and window catches.

At the news of this tragedy, Sybil and Grant hurry home, and only then do they hear of Cassie's pregnancy. Sybil's reaction is stunned disbelief, followed by a mood of nervous exaltation. In this state she lets fall an envelope addressed to Emma Marshall, an object seen by everyone present except her father. As Sybil drives with Grant towards their new home, the strangeness of her mood increases, and she puts forward a tentative theory that Cassie, far from young for a first pregnancy, might have killed Richard in a moment of mental instability. Forgetting that Grant was Richard's father, she goes on to hint that Duncan might suspect Cassie, and even be glad at the death of his putative child. Grant makes a protest at this nervous nonsense, but evil is running ever more wild in Sybil, and left alone with Dulcia, who has prepared a welcome for the couple, she whispers the same story. She adds the trimming that she can imagine that her father was involved in the dark deed with Cassie, and exonerates Grant from his affair with Alison on the grounds that he was suffering from Sybil's refusal of her own favours. A poor idea will have been given of Dulcia's capacity for mischief if it is a surprise to learn that she passes on all this vicious rigmarole to Beatrice Fellowes, after a series of hints has led Dulcia herself to the point where she is able to say ' "revelation is a duty" '.

'The duty of revelation' is carried even further when the Dorcas Society meets at the Burtenshaw's house. Against a background of flannel petticoats, Dulcia and Beatrice assist each other in spreading Sybil's suggestions among the company, giving them currency as slanderous rumours that have come into circulation by some spontaneous combustion of gossip. Dulcia even goes so far as to suggest that a pleasurable morbid shiver might be got from imagining that the rumour is true. Cold distaste for her proceedings displayed by the Smolletts penetrates Dulcia's ostrich-thick skin, to the extent that she is calling for a vote of confidence in the innocence of the Edgeworths when Gertrude Jekyll enters. Mrs Jekyll makes short shrift of Dulcia's attempt at back-pedalling. This behaviour shows that those who have suspected Duncan and Cassie of such a crime are near to it themselves, says Cassie's mother, and, as the five Edgeworths join the party, she goes on to inform them that their friends have just acquitted them of the death of their child after accusing them of it. Nance's comment is that it seems to have been a waste of time.

In the village shop Mrs Jekyll and Cassie meet Emma Marshall, who they see to be changing money orders from an envelope ressembling the one dropped by Sybil. Marshall is about to be married, and, in a mood of kindly congratulation, Cassie and Gertrude take her back to the Edgeworths' house, with the idea of giving her some of Richard's belongings. As things have worked out Cassie's unjust dismissal of Marshall has led to her own marriage with Duncan, by way of Marshall's vengeful revelation of Alison's adultery. Cassie has had a somewhat guilty feeling about her ruthless behaviour to

Marshall, but her reparatory kindness leads to yet another revelation. Gretchen, listening to Marshall's footsteps going up to a floor higher than the nursery had been in her day, takes Cassie with her to the room where Richard died. Confronting Marshall with the inescapable evidence that she knew the situation of the changed nursery, and the position of the gas taps, installed only recently, Gertrude's case against Richard's killer is complete. Marshall admits the receipt of an anonymous letter, thick with money, a letter telling her exactly what she must do. Further she admits that it was from Sybil that she received an earlier letter, urging her to take revenge by exposing Richard's true parentage.

In the drawing-room Marshall's guilt is explained to Duncan. And Marshall repeats to him the confession that shows Sybil to have been the instigator of the nurse's first offence. Sybil falls fainting onto a sofa, but Cassie's concern to help her is stopped by Mrs Jekyll. Sybil, Cassie's mother says, looked round for a soft fall before she fainted, as a way out of the awkward place in which she finds herself from her early doings coming to light, ' ". . . and few of us like that." Gretchen's tone was almost kind.'

Sybil, who has inherited Duncan's ability to talk her way out of a bad situation, explains that she was led to reveal Richard's illegitimacy by the idea that Alison would be cast out by Duncan, but had not conceived that Almeric would accompany Alison. With a return of total self-command, Sybil can even go on to speculate as to who could have planned Richard's death to their own benefit, scattering suspicion on her father and the Jekyll's as if she held a spray gun of slander in her hand. But her last defence goes down when Gertrude tells her exactly how Sybil accomplished the suborning of Marshall, from selling her brooch to raise money to making the envelope, though this is told in an aside unheard by Duncan. Marshall, promised her liberty by Gretchen in exchange for her confession, leaves the house and the story, which the Edgeworths are left to finish as best they may.

To sum up the situation, Duncan is alone in regarding Sybil as no more than an unkind betrayer of a secret. This gives him grounds for protest at Grant's insistence on separating from Sybil, who is driven to take refuge with Duncan's sister Maria. Duncan maintains that Grant, with his record, has no business to be censorious, but Nance blocks this protest by telling her father that he cannot arrange what his daughters do, for if he could things would be different. It is also Nance who urges on Duncan that each day should be lived by itself, and Duncan closes the chapter with a cry that he, an old man, has no peace, that it has all been too much.

Had the book ended on this note of defeat it would be difficult to quarrel with such a termination, leaving the Edgeworths floundering in a morass of trouble, from which no rescue appears possible. On a first reading it is hard to see how even Compton-Burnett's reserves of technical skill could take the story many stages further. What, the reader might well think, could be the amalgam which would reunite a family split by revelations of such evil-doing in one of its members? What bridge could be thrown across the abyss separating Sybil from her kin? The author knew the answer. It was the passion for an inheritance that has sent Sibyl beyond the family pale. Another inheritance is needed to bring her back within its bounds.

In the meantime Gretchen dies, apologising for the burden her keep has been to her son Oscar, and with her last breath admitting her preference for Cassie. Just after these last sharp words have been spoken, Beatrice Fellowes, with Dulcia as her lieutenant, arrives bringing religious counsel. As Cassie remarks, Mrs Jekyll has died in the nick of time. Duncan's sister, Maria, has also died, but there is not time to hear of the startling new terms of her will before Oscar inquires if

Duncan will agree to his proposing to Nance. This scene takes place over a game of cards, a rare relaxation for Compton-Burnett gentlemen, and Duncan comes as near to self-criticism as he ever reaches. He says he had hoped for more for Nance, though he does not know why ' "when she has seen nothing and nobody" '.

The results of Sybil's attendance on her Aunt Maria are revealed to her family in a concise letter. As a reward for Sybil's care her aunt has left her fortune to her niece, instead of dividing it between her nephews and nieces in proportion of two to one. Sybil has been dealt a strong hand and plays it faultlessly. If she returns to her home she will share twelve hundred a year with Grant, while Cassie's child, if a boy, will receive eight hundred, and Nance, as a daughter, half that sum. If she is obliged to live apart she will keep the entire fortune.

While the question of Sybil's future is still in debate, Oscar is able to announce to the meeting of the Dorcas Society that Cassie has given birth to a son. Miss Burtenshaw and Miss Fellowes are thrown into a state of acute sexual anticipation by this news, visions of other, late-in-time maternities rising in their imaginations. These fantasies are ephemeral, and fade at Oscar's announcing his engagement to Nance.

' "A wish of mine has come true, that the lady of the rectory should be taken from our midst," said Miss Burtenshaw, with briskness and truth.'

Duncan treats Grant and Nance's acceptance of Sybil's offer of herself and her fortune as a matter of course, and, in face of this attitude, Grant finds that he cannot tell his uncle the true cause of his separation from Sybil. When Grant finds that he cannot force further suffering on his uncle, the others can only acquiesce in the return of Sybil. With extreme objectivity in contemplating the nature of a former pupil, Cassie remarks that Sybil's moral sense had never been normal. Perhaps this lack of self-criticism in her failure to inculcate the moral sense lacking in Sybil makes Cassie a more suitable mate for Duncan than might, at first, be supposed. Always truthful about herself, Nance says she finds that her natural affection is asserting itself at the prospect of meeting Sibyl, or she prefers to imagine it is affection, because that sounds better than the avarice which she feels about the inheritance she owes to her sister.

Making an unsual display over the celebration of William's christening, in conjunction with Sibyl's return, Duncan is thrown into his old overbearing ways by some awkward comments from Nance. Having collided with Cassie in striding from the room, Duncan passes his third wife without a word. Cassie is, however, equal to the familiar situation, recommending her stepdaughter to keep out of Duncan's way until the guests arrive, because no man can be himself before guests. At last, Nance says, he has a wife who knows him, and Cassie agrees, adding that it seems unfair that Duncan does not know her in return, but to complain of being misunderstood is absurd.

In this spirit Cassie braces Nance to face the meeting with Sibyl, though she cannot, herself, avoid a nervous start, when Sibyl takes William, the new heir, in her arms. At dinner Duncan shows that his old gloomy personality is not dead, and this reversion to an earlier time of oppression draws Sibyl and Grant together. With Nance, they drift to the schoolroom where their former conspiracy, equally compounded of obsession with Duncan and mockery of him, is revived once again. It is Duncan who closes the book by remarking that he is always there with a necessary word, and that his family is there to learn from him.

Although not the longest of Compton-Burnett novels *A House and Its Head* may be called the richest both in the depth of its study of character and emotion, and in the wit that never fails to shine out in the darkest hours. On occasion the pressure of what a family can be brought to accept is carried to the exact point beyond which the roof would no longer hold. It is this mixture of pressure and relaxation that carries the story over such awkward, unanswered questions as to whether Doctor Smollett, on learning the truth about Richard's death, might not have felt it his duty to bring the law into the matter. Or how could track be kept of Marshall, though she is anyway in a wonderful position to practise life-long blackmail of the Edgeworths? Miss Fellowes and Miss Burtenshaw may rejoice in their secret hearts that neither has been preferred by Oscar, but there remains the problem of Dulcia. Unless she is transformed, Dulcia will be only too likely to continue to work off her pent-up sexual urges by referring to old scandals in public. Duncan's last speech leaves the reader with the prospect that he will continue to bully and harass his family. That Ellen's death may have been hastened by his callousness, that his passion for Alison has led to tragedy, that his daughter Sybil can threaten and betray, none of these factors have any influence on his own self-regard. As head of his house, Duncan also feels that money is his rightful possession, and, as Nance remarks, he would not have been able to support the loss of the eight hundred a year, due to be forfeited by his son William had Sibyl not been readmitted to the family.

' "Eight hundred a year extra on the wrong side might have been the last straw. I should indeed hardly call it a straw." ' said Nance.

Money is important in many of these novels, but in no other does a sudden shower of gold act as so strong a lubricant in the joints of the family machine. As a mechanic might strip an engine the author can take a family apart, and then, often in the face of wild improbability, reassemble the machine so that such families as the Edgeworths can continue their progress.

8

THE PRACTICE OF

LITERATURE

Although the ambition to write occurs among the characters of earlier books (*Pastors and Masters*, *Brothers and Sisters*, *Men and Wives*) it is in *Daughters and Sons* that the author, for the first time, constructs a plot that depends on literary efforts, both published and remunerative. The one small book which had to serve so many in *Pastors and Masters*, the unproductive 'writing' which was an alibi for two of the Staces in *Brothers and Sisters*, and the poems of Jermyn Haslam, published at his father's expense in *Men and Wives*, hardly represent a solid literary achievement. Literature at once comes into its own at the beginning of *Daughters and Sons*, when Sabine Ponsonby, a grandmother ruling harshly over her narrow domestic kingdom, complains that her second granddaughter, France, has filled her own room with rubbish. This rubbish is a book, whose writing gives France some outlet, in a life which has no prospect except a future of continuous abuse by Sabine for the burden of feeding grandchildren. Her elder sister, Clare, does not even have the solace of artistic creation, and the dull tone of her skin is a symptom of the *accidie* that possesses her, although she has a will strong enough to refuse the dose of medicine which her grandmother persistently measures out for her.

Sabine's insults to her grandsons' tutor have recently

caused him to leave the house, so Chilton and Victor are supposedly working on their own for entrance to a university. Chilton's verbal bullying of his younger brother is his form of holding his own in relation to his grandmother, but the bullying is mild compared with that which causes suffering, intense but suppressed, in *Parents and Children*. Victor has also some compensation in his consciousness of his own good looks and by joining his youngest sister, Muriel, in mocking the child's governess. The mother of this family has died at Muriel's birth, and although continually rebuked by her grandmother for giggling and yawning, she has enough hereditary wit and malice to give Miss Bunyan, the governess, a tough time.

John Ponsonby, father of the family and a novelist of some fame, has been consoled in his widowerhood by his sister Hetta's devotion. The intensity of Hetta's feeling has reduced her brother to a state of neurotic depression, coinciding with a falling off in his literary popularity. The prospect of the return home of her son and daughter gives Sabine an opportunity to toss an insult at Miss Bunyan by telling her that her company at dinner would be superfluous. Sabine's natural contempt for an employee has been increased by her knowledge, gained from steaming open Miss Bunyan's correspondence, that the governess represents herself as a cherished member of the household.

With the return of Hetta Ponsonby, a second domestic tyrant takes the field, though between Sabine and her daughter there is a relationship in which love and admiration play their part. Alone in her family, Hetta has no fear of Sabine so that disputes over the boundaries of domestic responsibility are fought vigorously rather than venomously. Hetta continuously reminds her family of her sacrifices on their behalf, but the author's view of self-sacrifice had changed since the days when she allowed a kind of purification to descend on Dolores from her immolation on the altar of family exaction. Overhearing her nephews and nieces discussing self-sacrifice, Hetta requires Victor to explain their conclusions. Victor replies, ' "That self-sacrifice is a bad thing for the person who makes it and tends to be regretted." ' This chilly philosophy is well illustrated later in the novel by the further deterioration in Hetta's abrasive personality.

Miss Bunyan's hearty appetite, and her habit of eating supplementary snacks, in her own room have already been the subject of acid comment from Sabine and unkind mockery from Muriel and Victor. Suitably enough, the breaking point comes at breakfast on Sunday, when Miss Bunyan gives notice. This has such a liberating effect on her manner towards her employer that Sabine resorts to ever more insulting reproofs, which, in the middle of luncheon, cause Miss Bunyan to declare that she will eat no more under Sabine's roof. It is, as Victor says, Miss Bunyan's triumph that she leaves in the middle of a meal, with Sabine's hands actually poised to carve the chicken.

Before another occupant for the painful position of Muriel's governess can be engaged, an entertainment takes place in the village. The organiser is the vicar of the parish, Doctor Chaucer, who happens also be the maternal uncle of Miss Bunyan. Secretly, he has arranged with France, her brothers and elder sister that part of her novel should be presented as a play, as her father has refused to take the work seriously enough to read it. John Ponsonby follows the play with interest for its literary promise, but he is thrown into a state of nervous jealousy when he discovers that his favourite daughter is the author. France returns her father's affection with sufficient force to forgive his churlish regret that it was not one of his sons who had creative talent. As her brother Chilton remarked earlier, ' "Though he slay you, yet will you trust in him." '

The entertainment of which the play is the centre brings together the two local families with which the Ponsonbys have neighbourly relations. The more important consists of giant middle-aged twins, Doctor Stephen Marcon and his sister Charity, whose work is the writing of books which she gets out of the British Museum. Their nephew Alfred has been engaged by Sabine as a tutor for her grandsons, his success in this office being surpassed by his success as a manipulator of Sabine's moods. Alfred's deft flattery has so charmed his employer that, at their first interview, she has been heard to assure him that good living is not neglected in her house, a remark astonishing to any of her former employees.

Less essential to the story than the Marcons are the Seymour family, Rowland a widowed baronet, Evelyn his son, and his spinster sister Jane. Miss Seymour is a type that is to be developed in later books, a single woman who keeps house for a male relation. Some of the later specimens contribute little more than a vague chaperonage for unmarried daughters, but Jane Seymour is so entranced with her position as a companion to two grown men that she has little interest to spare for anyone but herself. She does, however, provide Miss Marcon with a sparring partner, when the latter wishes to discuss the tribulations of three generations of Ponsonbys.

Having read France's novel, her father hesitates between acknowledging its merits, and facing the possibility that his own declining sales might be further reduced by the advent of a fresh young writer of the same name. His attitude is unlovable, but, in explaining his situation, he unconsciously gives sound professional advice on writing which France is intelligent enough to act upon. The revised work is sent to a publisher under the name of 'Edith Hallam', this concealment of France's identity under a *nom de plume* being suggested by the name's owner, who is yet another governess for Muriel. It is hoped thus to protect France's correspondence with a publisher from Sabine's prying, a foolish underestimation of the matriarch's practised skill in opening and resealing envelopes.

Lending France her name is only one of the ways that Edith Hallam makes her mark on the household. The quality of her spirit is demonstrated by her willingness to make do with the lesson books already in the schoolroom, experience having taught her that ' "Wanting new books is resented more than many graver things." ' Edith also meets Hetta in a battle of words and remains in possession of the field. Her predecessor, Miss Bunyan, is now installed as housekeeper to her uncle Doctor Chaucer, which has brought him to decide that a wife might provide him with comforts beyond the scope of a niece. His proposal to Edith is led up to by telling her that what he has in mind would transcend her furthest dreams. She replies, ' "What can it be? I thought you were going to propose to me. But that has nothing to do with my dreams." ' This scene of adroit refusal takes place at a dinner-party during which John Ponsonby has announced that a grateful, but anonymous, reader has sent him a gift of one thousand pounds. Although Sabine has caused embarrassment by suddenly saying aloud among her guests, ' "Are they never going?" ' she is fully able to take her customary keen interest in any mysterious correspondence. It is obvious that she will be active in stripping anonymity from her son's benefactor.

The reader learns the secret when Hetta reads out an advertisement of a novel by an 'Edith Hallam', which has won a prize of two thousand pounds. Edith's denial of any connection is accepted as true by Hetta and John, but Sabine, from her daily scrutiny of the post, has remarked that letters from a publisher's office have been delivered for Muriel's governess. With an assumption of aged weakness, she orders some tea and, by its help, steams open one such letter. Falling into a pit of her own digging, she fails to pierce the arrangement which shields France's authorship, and presumes that the gift of one thousand pounds has been sent by Edith as a token of admiration not purely literary. It seems to Sabine that Edith may be converted from an expensive employee to an additional source of family income. Although Hetta catches her mother in the act of tampering with the letter to Edith, she accepts Sabine's far from convincing explanation, but Hetta is soon to find that her mother's love for her will not prevent ruthlessness in pursuit of an illusory advantage to the family.

Hetta's discovery of 'Edith Hallam's' prize-winning novel has threatened France's secret, but France refuses to agree that the moment for revelation has come. Turning down this suggestion made by her fellow-conspirators, she says that she will not have her father made a butt because he has been deceived. Furthermore, she will have the matter kept a secret for ever, and she will give her father the second thousand pounds if she so wishes.

' "What words are these that escape the door of your lips?" said Chilton.

"Bring forth men children only!" said his brother.

"She had better bring forth brain-children. It would be better for the family," said Clare.

"Can people decide what kind of children they bring forth—have?" said Muriel. "I thought they couldn't."

"You are the one who is right," said Edith.

Muriel looked gratified, but hardly surprised that such information was not general.'

These quotations, from the Psalms and from *Macbeth*, give an edge to the conversation of the young Ponsonbys, whose words can be their own, King David's or Shakespeare's as seems fit at the moment. In addition, the delicacy with which Muriel's acquaintance with human physiology is set forth marks the beginning of the author's exploration into the intricacies of children's thoughts. In later books, such as

Parents and Children, or *Manservant and Maidservant*, the climax will often lie in the children's hands, and their elders are betrayed or saved by their actions.

With the perception that her son's struggle against Hetta's domination may lead him to welcome marriage as an escape, Sabine tells him her interpretation of the situation as she believes it to be, pressing on him that only deep love could have led Edith to make such a stupendous gift. John accepts his mother's ill-founded assurance that Hetta's words will break no bones. The power of Sabine's personality gives an hypnotic force to her wishes, stirring sexual feelings in both John and Edith. With an unusually direct acknowledgement of glandular turbulence in women, it is also mentioned that Edith's age makes her particularly susceptible to John's approach. Muriel's question as to whether her father and Edith will have any children is answered by Sabine with a directness ascribed by the author to Sabine's 'pre-Victorian youth'. Edith, Muriel's grandmother says, is not young enough. By Compton-Burnett standards Sabine was rash, for Edith is stated to have a birth certificate to prove she is only forty-six, and Cassie (*A House and its Head*) contributes a vital part to the plot by producing an heir having married in her early forties. (An even more extreme example of late breeding is to be found in *Daughters and Sons* where Eleanor Sullivan has given birth to her ninth child at the age of forty-five.)

Muriel's question about Edith's possible fertility occurs when the news of their father's second marriage is broken to his children. This follows a scene when even Sabine's iron nerve flinches at the ordeal of warning Hetta that she will be displaced by Edith. Receiving the news with the cosmic anger she shows when displeased, Hetta insults Edith as a social inferior, obliged to earn her living, and taunts her brother with his grief-stricken dependence on herself in the early days

of his widowerhood. Sabine's own fury breaks out when she hears her grandchildren speculating among themselves about Hetta's future, supplanted, as Hetta is, in a household which she has always maintained it needed her special genius to manage. Like a witch riding out on a storm, Sabine fulminates shrilly that her grandchildren should know how to treat their aunt with respectful gratitude, ' ". . . without my having to browbeat and bully you as if you were idiots or savages—"
"Grandma's view of the suitable treatment of the simple and afflicted invites criticism," said France.'

Hetta salvages her pride by assuring Doctor Chaucer (observed by Muriel to stare increasingly at Hetta) that her brother's marriage was something she had always predicted. But an opening for revenge comes to Hetta with the arrival of the second instalment of France's prize money. Sabine lets out some senile ramblings of gratitude towards Edith, revealing to her new daughter-in-law that she owes her marriage to John's belief that she was the anonymous benefactress. Having remarked the shock to Edith of this realization, Hetta pieces the evidence together, to find that Sabine and John have deluded themselves, and that France is both the author of the book and the giver of the money. Unable to resist the power given by this knowledge, Hetta is probing round the secret when Miss Blake, the latest governess to be exposed to the hazards of educating Muriel, interrupts the scene by desiring to leave immediately. Her reason is that Doctor Chaucer has proposed to her, and in his ardour has advanced too far in the assumption that he would be accepted. Hetta dismisses this story as a spinsterish fantasy, but she cannot blind herself to Sabine's increasing affection for Alfred Marcon, the boy's tutor, and to her brother's growing attachment to the wife he has married for mercenary reasons.

Suffering from these blows to her pride, Hetta disappears, leaving a note which indicates suicide. Sabine's wails of abuse at her family for allowing Hetta to reach this state add a burden to the hours of unfruitful search. Gradually, however, the family discover that the household duties of which Hetta made both a parade and a mystery can be carried out in her absence. To Sabine this is yet another insult to the memory of her daughter, and she is delivering a tirade on this theme when Hetta walks into the dining-room. The breakfast table becomes the scene of yet another power struggle, but although Hetta reconquers some territory she has lost her hold over her brother's work.

It has been mentioned earlier that Sabine actually expires at the dinner-table, at a party given, it might seem, to shorten a life already shaken by Hetta's faked suicide. The last attack is brought on by another loss of control on Hetta's part. The only person to mourn Hetta's supposed death and to rejoice at her return is her mother, but when Hetta spits out the truth about France's book the pile-up of emotion finishes Sabine. With her last look at life Sabine sees that Hetta is provided for, Doctor Chaucer taking her to himself in the satisfaction that her betrayal of family secrets has brought Hetta down to his level.

The guests, surprisingly unaffected by witnessing a death, find themselves able to discuss France's literary success. This leads to asking Hetta how he managed to discover that France, and not Edith, was the author. Hetta's half-exasperated reply contains deflating ideas familiar to all practitioners of literature. She had never believed, she says, in another 'Edith Hallam'. She had assumed that Edith had been shy about it, as authors are, though the shyness is incomprehensible as no one gives authors a thought. She adds that books that attract attention ought to be read. In this she is warmly supported by Miss Marcon, whose own books are brain-children begotten and brought forth in the British Museum Reading Room. She must, she says, expect people to read her books, otherwise why does she write them? And she does not read other people's books, which, after all, are not extracted from books already published as are Miss Marcon's own books. This is behaviour that keeps down sales. Miss Marcon concludes that ' "Hetta is the best of us" '.

Miss Marcon's approach to the financial aspect of authorship is essentially practical, and Hetta deserves her praise for, whatever her motives, actually buying France's book. But the financial difficulties of the Ponsonbys seem to take a turn for the worse when there is a rumour, leaked from the office of the local lawyer, that Sabine has left her fortune to Alfred Marcon. This breach of professional confidence has been organised by Evelyn Seymour, whose inordinate dislike of Alfred is stimulated by the idea that Alfred will be forced to give up the legacy, and so have neither money nor credit.

Faced with the news, Alfred decides to keep half the money and propose to Clare, knowing that her distaste for her home would make her welcome even him as a rescuer. Evelyn owns that he can hardly bear the situation which his leaking of the news has brought about, because had Alfred heard of his good fortune suddenly, in public, he would have felt obliged to return all the money to the assembled Ponsonbys. When he is faced with this situation, Alfred's estimate that Clare will accept him proves to be accurate. He rebuffs attempts, ranging from the autocratic to the wheedling, by which various Ponsonbys seek to convey that it is his duty to renounce the entire fortune. Alfred sticks to his terms, half the Ponsonbys' kingdom, with Clare thrown in, and Clare is prepared to throw herself. The bubble of Alfred's future bursts when Sabine's will is read after her funeral. The misapprehension has come from Alfred's name having replaced Hetta's as an executor, a change made by Sabine after her daughter's faked suicide. For Clare, however, another escape route opens; she is immediately sought as a wife by Sir Rowland Seymour, thirty years older, but one of Compton-Burnett's gentler baronets. This proposal is a surprise to Chilton and Victor. To their fraternal eyes it is astonishing that two men have offered themselves and all they had to their sister. ' "It is fortunate that the match is as suitable as it is," said Edith, "considering that she always accepts the men." '

The story ends with Stephen Marcon's prophecy that breakers are in front not behind. The very last words are with Miss Bunyan, who has returned to the task of teaching Muriel, to find that her pupil has not lost her habit of giggling nor has the governess herself lost her appetite which is the cause of the laughter.

Daughters and Sons is unusual among Compton-Burnett's books in that there is no actual criminal among the characters, and no sexual irregularity takes place, although John Ponsonby's relationship with his sister Hetta has sailed close to incestuous shores. The same relationship of a writer and a devoted sister-secretary will be met again in *A God and his Gifts*, but in that later work Hereward Egerton is so busy with the seduction of every woman who joins the family that he has only time to mention, in passing, his regret that the blood tie prevents his sister Zillah from being sexually accessible. By comparison, Hetta Ponsonby's contempt for her brother is understandable, when, having discovered John's motive for marrying Edith, Hetta says, ' "They are so paltry these sums of money which mould your life." '

At moments, the minor characters of *Daughters and Sons* appear to be slightly out of focus. For example the giant twins, Stephen and Charity Marcon have something of the unbelievable quality of the giraffe which they resemble. The neurotic Alfred Marcon needs the foil of Evelyn Seymour, but Jane Seymour is an extreme type of the superfluous spinster with whom the author had an inclination to populate the background of her family groups. Far stronger are the portraits of the sons and daughters, particularly that of the child Muriel, a forerunner of the splendidly achieved schoolroom and nursery parties of later books. Victims of both Sabine and Hetta, the young Ponsonbys are not without a spirit of rebellion, though Hetta's belief in her own myth is too strong to allow more than a passing sneer at symptoms of mutiny. On the other hand when Sabine surprises her grandson Chilton wearing her own cloak and bonnet, his forehead fringed with horse hair plucked from the sofa, she ignores the take-off of herself, and merely reproves him for spoiling the furniture. Sabine is not the only one among Compton-Burnett tyrants to know the value of keeping their subjects off balance by lapses into leniency.

9

GENEROSITY BRINGS PAIN

If there is only one young bride and no young bridegrooms in
Daughters and Sons, in Compton-Burnett's next book, *A
Family and a Fortune*, no marriages are accomplished, or
planned, between anyone under fifty. The young of the
Family 'see no one and go nowhere'. Tyranny has only one
practitioner, and only one victim; active crime is again in
abeyance and it is the Fortune of the book's title which gives
the novel its impetus. There is an unresolved tragedy in the
person of Aubrey, the youngest son of the Family. He is a
wizened changeling, his stunted physique perhaps due to his
being late-born to his mother, a speculation not, however, put
forward by the author.

In their handsome decaying house the Gavestons assemble
for breakfast, one of the author's gifts being her literary
ability to approach the day's first meal from an ever-fresh
angle. Blanche, the mother of the family, although riled
by her daughter Justine's officiousness over pouring out coffee,
has none of the tortured reaction to the normal ambitions of
her children which made Harriet Haslam (*Men and Wives*)
such a painful breakfast table companion. Her husband,
Edgar, is unusually forbearing, both in his marriage and in
his dealings with his children. The eldest and only daughter,
Justine, might be described as a virtuous Dulcia Bode (*A
House and Its Head*), equally a 'blunderbuss', but untouched

by any sinister tendency to make mischief. Mark, the eldest son and heir, has the occupation accorded to that position in a Compton-Burnett landed family. Clement, the remaining brother, has a harsh, unsympathetic character. With an academic future before him, he seems destined to be the gloomiest of dons. Dudley Gaveston, Edgar's younger brother, lives a life of dependence under the family roof, their fraternal devotion being a more than adequate recompense to the dependant and to the provider.

Aubrey, at the age of fifteen, is alone in realising that he is both too old and too backward to follow his elder brothers to Eton, an unusually definite statement as to where a Compton-Burnett family finds its education. Edgar and Dudley have also been educated in Henry's Holy Shade, but they both declare that they have forgotten everything learnt there. Justine insists that an education at ' "the greatest school in the world" ' must have left its trace, but Aubrey, whose protection is self-mockery, suggests that it will not matter if he cannot have this educational benefit; it will only be a shorter cut to knowing nothing.

Blanche's insomnia is less intense than Harriet Haslam's and her family treat it more lightly, Justine remarking that her mother makes up for a bad night in the afternoon. Blanche shows the normal human annoyance at being told she had been heard to snore when resting on her bed, and Justine's maddeningly good-natured insistence that her mother was both asleep and snoring, is only checked by Edgar's kind intervention. Clement asks why it is impossible to learn that no one ever snores under any circumstances. ' "I wonder how the idea of snoring arose" said Mark.'

The decay of their ancestral home lays a burden on Edgar Gaveston's income, and this is now augmented by an application from Blanche's father and her unmarried sister Matty to rent an empty lodge for the lowest sum that the estate

can bear. Impossible as it is to refuse this request, the prospect
daunts Blanche's family for reasons other than financial loss.
Oliver Seaton, at eighty-seven, is not unduly inactive or
mentally aged, Compton-Burnett octogenarians being on
the whole a healthy lot, who, when they quit life's stage, do
so with obliging celerity. But Blanche's sister Matty is a more
difficult problem. Her grossly inflated idea of herself as
beautiful and gifted, with a destiny marred by lameness due
to a riding accident, makes her awkward company in the
family, and a slave-driver to Miss Griffin her companion.
Blanche rejects Justine's suggestions that she may disagree
with her sister, brushing them aside with the honest simplicity
that is the charm of her nature. The same quality leads her
to protest at her elder sons' teasing remarks that the sight
of Aubrey may be a shock to the elderly and invalid. Aubrey
is due to leave the house with Mr Penrose, his tutor, but
before he goes he has to suffer the championship of his
mother and reproofs by his sister to his brothers, an agony
lived with but continually renewed.

On their arrival in the gate-lodge, Oliver and Matty let lose
their depression in verbal tit-for-tat, Oliver criticising Matty's
demeanour towards Miss Griffin, and Matty retaliating that
dinner will, in due course, alleviate Oliver's ill-humour.
Matty's complaints that her family have not come in person
to welcome these newly arrived poor men at the gate, change
only in tone with the advent of Blanche. Finding it hard to
accept her reduced condition, Matty snipes at her sister for
the economies which inhibit unrestricted entertaining at the
big house, her own lavish house-keeping having played its
part in the debts that have brought her in poverty to her
sister's door-step.

With the entry of Miss Griffin, exhausted but taught by
Matty that the sedentary suffer more than the active, the
room begins to fill up. Edgar and Dudley's arrival further

emphasize the small scale of the lodge, and the addition of Justine seems 'to render the room at once completely full'. Putting her best foot into a delicate situation, Justine praises the snugness of the cottage parlour, and, undeterred by her mother and her aunt who, for different reasons take exception to her description, continues to develop the theme. She looks forward with pleasure to her middle-age in just such a cottage, or even this same one, where she will rule in her tiny kingdom, doing what good she can, while her brother Mark reigns in the family home. Justine inquires of the company whether they do not see this as an alluring prospect.

' "Yes, it sounds very nice," said Miss Griffin, who thought that it did, and who was perhaps the natural person to reply, as the arrangements involved the death of most of the other people present.'

Later in the evening Matty's viper nature looses itself in a barely sane attack on Miss Griffin. Her subsequent attempt to restore the appearance of friendliness fails to work on her companion, who, perhaps stimulated by the move, at last sees clearly the thirty years of her slavery, with nothing of hope or pleasure behind her or before her.

A family dinner party to welcome Matty and her father brings no addition to the family circle, except one elderly couple, Mr and Mrs Middleton. Their contribution to the party, and indeed to the development of the story, is small. Mr Middleton has once wished to write, but, retiring from being a schoolmaster to live on his wife's means, he has been unable to decide on a subject. His dimness is unrelieved, but Mrs Middleton's is illuminated by the intensity of her curiosity, a quality never underestimated in value by the author, and in this case burning with a particularly strong flame. The dinner party is another occasion of suffering to Aubrey. Justine has been expatiating on the bad fit of her new magenta gown, which does sound truly horrible, when

Dudley kindly suggests that it could be transformed into a dressing-gown. Unguardedly, Aubrey lets out that he is in the habit of inspecting people's dressing-gowns to admire their gay colours. He then has to lie his way out of an inquisition into his thoughts by Justine, being 'reluctant to explain that he had been imagining future daughters for himself and deciding the colours of their dressing gowns'.

This conception of a growing child finding compensation for the malaise of puberty in visions that would cease to be comforting if exposed to the light, will be found again, more fully developed, in *Parents and Children*, where only two of the nine children escape emotional agonies. Aubrey's misfortunes include the reinforcement of his natural mother by the smothering attentions of Justine, with no counter-balance from his father. Indeed Edgar has only kindness and concern for his children, needing patience in addition to support the discomfort of Justine's attentions in her self-constituted role as her father's darling.

It is Justine's determination to perform acts of kindness, in spite of their dubious benefit to the recipients, which sends her, after dinner, to fetch Miss Griffin to join the company, in the face of a general feeling that the poor slave would be happier for a respite. Not only Miss Griffin joins the party. With a flourish, Justine introduces Maria Sloane, a friend expected by Matty, but who has arrived before the arranged date. Maria might be an older Alison Edgeworth (*A House and Its Head*) had Alison remained a spinster. A handsome, middle-aged woman, she is dressed with a kind of simplicity which some of the company see as costing more than elaboration, but Maria knew 'that when these two qualities are on the same level simplicity costs much less'.

Left alone together after the party the relationship, built by a lifetime of affection, between Dudley and Edgar is disturbed by Dudley's news that he has inherited a fortune, an income of two thousand a year, by the death of a godfather, aged ninety-six. The greatness of the age precludes grief, and even Oliver, when he hears the news, can, from the security of eighty-seven, call the deceased godfather ' "a very old fellow" '.

Dudley describes his own feelings as natural, proceeding as they do through shock, delight and excitement, to compunction at having so much, to worry that he should be thought to have even more, though at that moment he did not know how much reason there would be for this last sensation. He here refers to the arrival of Matty and her father, who, having received the news by way of Jellamy, the butler, and an errand boy, have come to congratulate Dudley on inheriting a quarter of a million. Had this been the case Dudley could hardly have made more generous arrangements, for by luncheon time on the day that the news is generally known he has pledged almost his entire income in repairs to the house and allowances to his brother's children. He is, himself, conscious of the unfairness of the arrangement he is making, in that it gives most to Clement, who will spend the money solely on himself, and the least to Justine, who will spend it on other people. Naturally it is Justine, and not Clement, who insists, with prescience, that should Dudley wish to change his way of life the allowances should cease and his income should return to him.

Only too soon, from the point of view of his family, Dudley behaves like a man of means and becomes engaged to Maria Sloane, who, as Aubrey points out, will now become an aunt and therefore be obliged to kiss Clement. Any question of returning the allowances to Dudley lies in abeyance for a while, because Blanche's lachrymose rejoicing at the news of the engagement turns out to be the early symptoms of pneumonia. Nursed by Miss Griffin, Blanche survives the crisis, only to succumb to a relapse, at a moment when Justine is in floods of untypical tears and Matty's self-assertion is particularly insensitive. Pneumonia is not, it should be said, specified, but the pattern of symptoms, days of fever followed by a crisis, is the same as that which gave Josephine Napier (*More Women than Men*) the opportunity to assist her nephew's wife Ruth out of this world. Later in *A Family and a Fortune* Dudley Gaveston has a narrow squeak from the same complaint.

Following Blanche's death, her family fail to be of consolation to her widower, increasingly depressed by the prospect of his brother's marriage and the loss it will bring. Justine, although not unduly cast down by her mother's deathbed inquiry if she is the beautiful daughter Blanche knew she would have or ' "the other one" ', finds herself inadequate in this predicament. Clement, however, observes that sympathy is developing between his father and Maria, and with the cunning of self-interest promotes a scheme by which Dudley absents himself, leaving Maria free to console Edgar. The plan works so brilliantly that, on coming home, Dudley in his turn is confronted by a double loss, for Edgar and Maria announce that they are now engaged to marry.

Dudley reverts to his position as the provedly generous uncle, restoring the allowances to his nephews and nieces. But he confides to Miss Griffin that he now likes Maria less than he did, because it seems so obvious of his former betrothed to have chosen the more eligible brother. Miss Griffin suggests that a widower with a family might not seem more eligible to everybody, to which Dudley replies that if Maria really prefers Edgar he likes her even less. These moments of confidence with Miss Griffin are suspected and resented by Matty, who, in her concentration on herself, cannot understand that it is her own maltreatment of Miss Griffin which leads Dudley to make his kind gestures.

Unhappily, the return of Edgar and Maria from their

honeymoon brings about the collapse of the brave front Dudley has maintained. What promises to be a peaceful beginning of a new phase of family life is disrupted by Matty's uninvited appearance. Clement's remark, that at one time his aunt would have been burnt as a witch, is capped by Aubrey's suggestion that his brother's tone betrays a yearning for the good old days, and emphasized by Mark's reflection that, on the other hand, witches always seem to have been innocent people. After Matty has withdrawn, leaving her trail of devastation, it becomes clear that Edgar and Maria have now reached a stage of intimacy together which excludes Dudley. His wounded spirit finds words to castigate Edgar for the cold-heartedness which has kept him from caring for his brother, his wife or his children. Still on the wave of this bitterness, Dudley leaves the home of all his life. As he walks through the snow he finds Miss Griffin shivering in the garden of the lodge, Matty having brought her evil mood to a climax by expelling her companion. In his stricken loneliness, Dudley proposes marriage to Miss Griffin, though even as he does so he understands that she has an irritating quality which might explain, without excusing, Matty's screams of nervous exasperation. Driven out though she has been, Miss Griffin retains the good sense to refuse Dudley's offer, which is eventually compounded for funds that will provide a cottage and an income. In the meantime shelter is found for Miss Griffin at the house of the Middletons, Mrs Middleton's passionate curiosity about her neighbours, receiving, on this occasion, perfect satisfaction.

The difficulty of explaining Dudley's absence at the breakfast table is made no easier for Edgar by the demeanour of Jellamy the butler. Jellamy has been servilely anxious to please Dudley at the first news of the inheritance, but this does not prevent him from aggravating the painful situation caused by Dudley's departure, without either taking luggage or leaving an address. Edgar and Maria are obliged to abandon their pretence that Dudley is taking a natural holiday when Matty is seen limping through the snow towards the house. She has arrived to announce that her father has died in his sleep, and, true to her nature, presents herself as the sufferer of ' "deep experiences" ' which, in spite of their constant recurrence, finds her completely vulnerable.

' "Losing her father when she is over sixty herself is not a startling one," said Clement.'

Matty sweeps aside some questions about Miss Griffin, who, she explains, has left her in a dark hour, another example of the strange happenings that allow Matty to declare herself to be a remarkable figure. Discovering Dudley's flight, she is able to equate this with Miss Griffin's defection, but only to her own satisfaction. General suspicion that Matty has surpassed herself in brutality towards Miss Griffin is increased when Jellamy, with barely disguised pleasure, intervenes with the news that Dudley has been seen escorting Miss Griffin through the snow, the lady being wrapped in Mr Dudley's overcoat. Matty's attempt to treat this as a truly comic episode fails, and Maria does not hesitate to declare the enormity of Matty's behaviour. Maria's attitude is a help to her in calming the tumult in Aubrey's mind. The boy is not only harrowed by the vision of Miss Griffin cast out into the snow, he is also torn between loyalty to his dead mother and the consciousness that he can charm his stepmother. He accepts her suggestion that there are times when one should not mind being thought callous, agreeing that ' "the heart knoweth" '.

This quotation from the Book of Proverbs, already used in *Daughters and Sons*, leaves the family still stuck in the bitterness which has led to Dudley's evasion. It is, eventually, the result of this flight and Dudley's carelessness of his own welfare that reunites the family. Once again Matty appears at the big house to announce that Dudley is lying near death

at a farmhouse twenty miles away. He has had the presence
of mind to send for Miss Griffin, before lapsing into an illness
like that which killed Blanche. Leaving Matty and Aubrey
to keep house, an incongruous pair, immobilised by lameness
and youth, the rest of the family gather round Dudley. Like
Blanche, among whose last words was a statement of how
much nicer a person she was than her sister Matty, Dudley,
approaching the crisis of his illness, broods aloud on his
feeling for his brother, greater than his feelings had ever been
for Maria. In her turn, Maria can assure him that Edgar
reciprocates.

The novel is rounded off by Dudley's convalescent return
to a home where rejoicing is an emollient in the awkward
encounter between Matty and Miss Griffin. With her habitual
self-assertion, Matty can even twist the news that Dudley is to
make Miss Griffin independent into a compliment to herself,
as the one who introduced Miss Griffin to her benefactor.
Among down-trodden companions Miss Griffin is the only
one allowed by the author to escape from thraldom, but then
she is the only companion to suffer physical ill-treatment.
Rightly, Aubrey inquires if the next person who is to depend
on his aunt for a home ought not to be told that it might
be in the garden.

A slight slip on the stairs by Dudley leads to his being
laid on the bed in Clement's room, an apartment usually
kept private by its owner. The final demoralising effect of
the Fortune on the Family is revealed when a cascade of gold
coins tumbles inadvertently from Clement's desk. Failing to
get Clement to explain the satisfaction derived from such
positive miserliness, Dudley refuses to go and rest on his own
bed. He cannot bear to be shut away from the impending
gossip.

' "It will be a beautiful family talk, mean and worried and
full of sorrow and spite and excitement. I cannot be asked to

miss it in my weak state. I should only fret." '

Like the receding shot at the end of a film, the last sight of
the Gavestons shows Dudley leaning on Edgar's arm as they
stroll away, reunited, into the sunshine.

In fact, it is the likeness and essential difference between
the two brothers which weaves the pattern of this book.
Dudley is never at a loss for an off-beat comment, which is
often at his own expense; he is impulsive and imaginative,
as opposed to Edgar, who is painstaking in his efforts to say
no more and no less than the truth. Edgar's gentleness to his
wife Blanche is matched by his patient acceptance of Justine's
pose as an adored only daughter. '. . . Justine threw her arms
about his neck and kissed him on both cheeks, a proceeding
which always seemed to him to take some time.' At the end
of the book Edgar, in his relief at Dudley's recovery, asks his
brother if his feeling for Maria is still powerful. Dudley is able
to answer that it is not, but adds that Edgar married Maria
too soon after Blanche's death. Edgar agrees, admitting that
he was unused to women's society, and that he thinks emotion
of one kind ' "may dispose the mind to others" '. Dudley says
that he wonders why people say they are unlike, when they
seem to be so much the same. ' "But grief for a wife is a
better emotion than excitement over money. Your second
feeling had a nobler foundation and deserved success." '

Success is, in fact, exactly what Edgar has, involuntarily,
achieved. Even the malice of Matty has been subdued by the
force of Maria's character, so that Edgar is left in unimpeded
enjoyment of the devotion of Dudley, who is to him the
Family, and of the Fortune, which Dudley, content in the
knowledge that he holds Edgar's heart, is prepared to pour
out for his brother's benefit.

10

NINE OLIVE BRANCHES

Once asked by a friend of a younger generation if she, the author, had ever wished for children, I. Compton-Burnett replied that she had not, but she had sometimes thought that she would have managed them better than some mothers whom she had observed. She had a sound basis for this belief. Throughout her novels the minds and motives of the children she describes are observed with a perception deeply original. In no other book, however, does she set herself such a formidable task as in *Parents and Children*. Here the reader is presented with a family of nine, born to parents who have the added handicap of living in the house of the family patriarch, Sir Jesse Sullivan. His wife bears the name of Regan given her by her father as a result of reading that Shakespeare's women were 'people of significance'. Regan has dealt with this handicap by observing that the name must have been in use before Shakespeare gave it villainous connotation. Unlike her namesake, she has devoted her life to loving her immediate family. As this has resulted in loving thirteen people, she may, the author observes, have loved more than the average number. The total of those Regan has loved is made up of her husband, a son and daughter deceased, her surviving son, Fulbert, and Fulbert's nine children. Her daughter-in-law Eleanor, being no blood relation, is not included in the number beloved by Regan, and this may be an element in Eleanor's discontent.

Parents and Children opens with Eleanor's complaint at a dependent life in a home that is not hers. This complaint comes inopportunely at a moment of family upheaval, for Fulbert is on the point of leaving for South America to attend to his father's business interests. Sir Jesse has spent some of his early life in that continent, and James, one of Fulbert's younger sons, tell his father that his grandfather says the trees and flowers were different from those in England. Fulbert's particular kind of sprightly egoism comes out when he replies that things can hardly be the same as when Sir Jesse was there, 'though the changes might hardly extend to the vegetation,' as the author remarks. His children, he says must wait for his return to learn details of South America.

Fulbert's imminent departure hangs like a fog over the house, his father alone refusing to moderate his attitude of domestic dictatorship. Sir Jesse's chief cause of complaint is the expense incurred by the education of his two eldest grandsons, Daniel, an extrovert, and Graham, a melancholic. The former has the habit of presenting the latter as a butt, without the geniality which softens Chilton's similar behaviour towards Victor in *Daughters and Sons*. Daniel's bullying is deprecated by Luce, the eldest daughter of the family and a less aggressive, and less philanthropic version of Justine Gaveston (A *Family and a Fortune*). To Sir Jesse, feeling no personal loss from little education, the sight of his grandsons at meals is an only too frequent reminder of the sums he has laid out on them. Apart from meals he shuns the company of these Cambridge undergraduates as being below his own standard. ' "We are all of us human or should be. In their case I begin to have doubt. Grinning and chattering like apes and costing like dukes!" '

Daniel and Graham have concluded that their grandfather's reiterated attacks on them as ducally expensive monkeys arise from the fact that they are male and adult, while none of the others of their parents' children are both. These others live upstairs in a schoolroom party composed of Isabel, Venice and James, while higher still there is a nursery group, Honor, Gavin, and finally Nevill, three years old and a determined clinger to the privileges of the last baby. In the schoolroom Miss Mitford, Mitta, conducts the education of the middle three of the family, attending primarily to her own comfort. In the nursery Hatton, the nurse, rules unquestioned, but allows her lieutenant, Mullet, the nursery-maid, certain rights of creative fantasy in dealing with her charges.

Mullet's serial account of her own childhood not only enlivens the tedium of hair-brushing and nursery walks, it can also be adapted to become a consolation when Honor and Gavin are faced with family crises. Mullet's childhood was passed, it appears in a house comparable to that which shelters Honor and Gavin. Her father, returning unexpectedly with ' "a peremptory ring" ' of the bell, finds his daughter, ' "his heiress" ', neglected by the household staff, whom he promptly dismisses. This mass sacking of domestics led to evil times in which Mullet found herself an impoverished orphan. Gavin asks if her father would have objected to Mullet becoming a nurse, to which Mullet replies that he had in one sense a gentleman's respect for useful work. ' "In another it would have broken his heart," said Mullet, hardly taking an exaggerated view, considering her parent's reaction to milder vicissitudes.'

The vicissitudes that now begin to overtake the Sullivan family are worthy of Mullet's imagination, though conveyed in less extreme language. The worst threat comes from the Cranmers, the only intimates of the Sullivans. Paul, the father, is a retired lawyer, who can keep a secret, even from Hope his second wife. Hope herself keeps up a flow of barbed remarks, mostly directed at her stepson Ridley, and at Faith, his sister. The latter's name may have encouraged a determination to do good in its owner, but Ridley Cranmer develops as a single complete villain, rather than the double martyr implicit in his cognomen. As well as being the target of her stepmother's darts, Faith suffers a defeat at the hands of the nursery children, when she attempts to persuade them of the cruelty of shooting live birds. Cruelty comes easily to Honor and Gavin, as Miss Pilbeam, their new nursery governess has had good reason to know.

In a damp cottage on the edge of the park, Sir Jesse has installed a family of three, Priscilla, Susan and Lester Marlowe, spinster sisters and a bachelor brother. They are an odd-looking trio, partly maintained by Sir Jesse, a friend of their dead parents in his South American days, but not received by him in his own house. Daniel and Graham, however, have a habit of dropping in to escape from pressures at home. Hope Cranmer brings her husband to call with the same object, but her efforts to escape are hampered by Faith's determination to keep everyone of her acquaintance under surveillance, which compels her to follow her stepmother with Ridley in tow. Consequently the four Cranmers are present when the Marlowes examine a photograph of their dead mother. This is their first sight of their maternal parent, in a portrait handed to them by Sir Jesse, when he paid a recent call to examine the Marlowes' accounts and urge economy on them. Addicted to probing other people's affairs, Faith discovers that Sir Jesse has never given the Marlowes a picture of their father, nor, as they seldom ask him questions, have they asked him for such a gift. Faith suggests that he would not mind a question on such a subject, but her father surprises her by saying that it might be no exception. This dialogue, and the fact, noted later in the same chapter, that Lester Marlowe and Graham Sullivan both have a squeak in their voices should be borne in mind as clues to later revelations.

Fulbert's actual departure is like the slow extraction of a tooth, but it is finally accomplished, with a parting charge to Ridley that, should Fulbert not return, Ridley will be his trustee. Left alone with her family, Eleanor continues her neurotic skirmishing, without the antidote of Fulbert's liveliness. Eleanor appears at her worst when, in spite of protests, she opens a letter addressed by Fulbert to Isabel, his favourite among his daughters. Isabel, in revenge, opens her father's letter to her mother and finds that the wording in both letters is identical. As Isabel says to her mother, in trying to make her daughter appear childish and foolish she has sacrificed her husband. In spite of this *débâcle*, Eleanor persists in asserting that her child's schoolroom is a happy establishment. She overlooks that the more sophisticated side of the girls' education is supplied by books Miss Mitford obtains for her own pleasure, and that James, frequently an ailing absentee from his day school, uses the same source, concealing his interest by artifices that suggest that books to him are objects and not reading matter.

This uneasy phase comes to an end when Ridley Cranmer receives a letter from Fulbert, who is lying at the point of death. Should no cable arrive, overtaking this letter, to tell of his recovery, the receipt of the letter must be considered as the announcement that Fulbert is no more. Regan is thrown into a passion of grief by the news, but the effect on Fulbert's father is more complex. His feelings send him, at length, to commune with the Marlowes, though his announcement that he is now a childless man subsequently turns out to be less than accurate. As always the Marlowes are uneasy when their patron sits gazing into the fire, as they are in the habit of supplementing the inadequate amount of coal sent them by Sir Jesse with wood purloined from his park under cover of dusk. In a nervous aside to her brother and sister, Priscilla says that, though people are supposed to see faces in the fire, she can only be afraid that Sir Jesse will see wood.

This mournful, but unusually friendly, visit from Sir Jesse is followed by a call from Ridley Cranmer. He is insufferably exalted in his position of trustee, and ominously curious about Fulbert's father's relations with the Marlowes. He is also full of praise for Eleanor Sullivan's demeanour, and even in her grief Lady Sullivan finds this interest in her son's widow a matter for suspicion and disapproval.

Upstairs the nursery-children are consoled by another instalment of Mullet's family history. They are fortunate, she says, in that they will continue in their own home, unlike a family of her own cousins, who, on the death of their father had to retrench and follow a ' "second-rate social round" ' in an atmosphere of ' "shabby gentility" '. Their lot was rendered harder because, ' "after an interview with the rather tyrannical cook," ' they were subjected to ' "a dose of cavalier treatment from the tradesmen instead of the accustomed respect" '.

When Faith, against Luce's advice, forces her way into the nursery, she finds that the three schoolroom children have also retired to the healing shelter of Hatton's care. The joint imaginations of Gavin and Nevill have transformed their father into an image of Sir John Moore, enabling them to conduct a military funeral with appropriate quotations.

' "Do you have a coffin?" said James . . .

"No," said Gavin, "Just his martial cloak around him." '

With no reward but a kindly word from Nevill, Faith withdraws before a positive attack from Gavin and a glacial silence from the others. Honor breaks the silence when Faith has shut the door.

' "Not a high type," she said.'

Shortly afterwards, the children have more reason to

comment on the Cranmer family. Ridley, having made himself agreeable by a game in the hall with a lion skin, leaves the younger children to assess the situation, while he goes for an interview with their grandparents. The air is heavy with apprehension, and Gavin, in particular, has an additional cause for misery as Honor, his life's comfort, is showing alarming signs of talking on equal terms with the schoolroom children. When Honor remarks that there are breakers ahead, Gavin can stand this alienation no longer. Quite deliberately, he gives his sister a kick, which she, equally deliberately returns, the exchange allows them to return to their normal relationship.

The storm signal of 'breakers ahead', a Compton-Burnett indication of coming matrimonial disturbances, is an advance warning of the engagement of Eleanor to Ridley. On their marriage they propose to retire to a house of their own in the village, a step for which Eleanor has pleaded in Fulbert's lifetime. The plan is regarded with relief by those of her children who can comprehend the benefits to be expected from their mother's withdrawal. Mullet, once again, supplies an appropriate anecdote from the annals of her family, though her gift for improvisation is stretched by questions from her listeners before she has worked out the line of her narrative. In the end she leaves them with a satisfactory picture of an aunt married to a second husband, a man with a sinister scar across his face, who cast a dark shadow over the family. Gavin presses to know what the man with the scar actually did, but from her greater sophistication Honor is prepared to accept that there are things children cannot be told.

Almost at once Ridley returns to the house to say that a rush of business will oblige him to ask that his wedding should take place in the course of the next few days, adding that he wishes he could rid himself of the idea that he was carrying off his bride.

' "Why does one dislike the term, bride, as applied to one's mother?" said Luce.

"There are several reasons and none of them can be mentioned," said Graham.'

On her last shopping expedition before her wedding, Eleanor is made uncomfortable by the persistence with which Gavin maintains that he has seen his father in the town. Attempts to reason away his delusion are met with stubbornness. Finally, alone with his grandmother, Gavin describes the details of the coat he has seen his father wearing. Then Regan realises that the boy is speaking the astounding truth, and drives fast to bring her son home.

This return of one supposed dead has an embarrassing aspect for Ridley, but Fulbert accepts his wife's fiancé's assurance that the letter announcing Fulbert's recovery and return had never been delivered. It might be argued that Fulbert's wish to avoid a shock to his family by putting up at the inn is a somewhat creaky contrivance, but it may be excused as an aberration of convalescence. That Eleanor had accepted Ridley as a husband is not made a matter of reproach by Fulbert, though Nevill shows some confusion at being required to accept again the father whom he had buried with, as he said, ' "Beat the drum and make a thunder noise." '

Ridley is doing his best to entertain Nevill with the contents of his pocket book, when a loose leaf from the book is filched by Gavin, who is becoming liberated from his usual dependence on Honor. Obviously methodical as a solicitor, Ridley has been unwise enough to set down on his list of wedding preparations a note that Fulbert would be at the inn in the town, adding that, having made Eleanor an unconscious bigamist, he, Ridley, would write when on honeymoon as if Fulbert's letter had only just reached him. Gavin, slipping into a space where a full-grown man cannot follow, reads this damning list aloud.

Ridley faces his exposure with the calm of someone who has gone too far, but who has still a trick up his sleeve. His declaration that had his scheme succeeded, Eleanor would have preferred to remain with him is greeted by Sir Jesse with a furious command to leave the house. Ridley goes, but on his way out he shows a photograph first to Sir Jesse and then to Regan, a photograph which shows Sir Jesse in a lover-like pose with, unmistakably, the 'mother of the Marlowes'.

At this further exposure, Luce herds the schoolroom children upstairs, on the grounds that they are of an age when they will be baffled by the sexual implications. James may well be baffled, but Venice is reassured that Isabel has profited enough from Miss Mitford's library books to be able to explain matters. As Fulbert takes Eleanor away to their sitting-room, he wishes the rest of the Cranmers and his children joy of what should be a wonderful gossip. In the course of this splendid survey of family skeletons it is revealed that Paul Cranmer, pitied by his wife for the tedium of sitting next to Sir Jesse, has been on such terms that not only has he known about the origin of the Marlowes, but has known, also, that Regan has guessed the secret. Even Sir Jesse is thought to have had something of a shock when his wife said a word to him on the subject of his bastards.

Ridley's final act of revenge is to spread the news of Sir Jesse's second family, so that there is no inhibition preventing Daniel and Graham from discussing their relationship with the Marlowes to the Marlowes themselves. It is realised that Luce has not been allowed to visit the cottage as a precaution, on Sir Jesse's part, against the possibility that she might fall in love with her half-uncle. He did not consider that his grandsons needed similar protection from their half-aunts, eccentric-looking and older than themselves. The conference is disturbed by the delivery of a note from Hope Cranmer, regretting that she could not bear to join a party in which she would be the only person not related to Sir Jesse. 'I still hope that it may be found out that I am, . . .'

Priscilla Marlowe remarks that it may seem odd that Sir Jesse has appeared on his habitual walk past the cottage, but then he has had no shock of revelation. Urged by her sister, Susan, Priscilla stands at the window, to see if he will modify his distant maner. In the last sentence of the book Sir Jesse remains consistent, with a glance towards his daughter he merely raises his hat and continues his walk. Sir Jesse may have feet of clay, but they are firmly bedded in cement.

Although the last two chapters of *Parents and Children* are tense with excitement, climax building upon climax, the real strength, it would be not too much to say the beauty of the book, lies in the growth of the personalities of the younger Sullivans. Like all children they are explorers in territory occupied by incalculable and potentially hostile forces. Nevill, at three years old, is already given to fawning hypocritically on his mother, whose visits to the nursery he regards as tedious interruptions in his happy communion with Hatton the nurse. At their ages of nine and ten, Gavin and Honor sum up the situation by describing Nevill as one of the baser creatures.

' "If people knew we had a baser creature, we should be prosecuted," said Honor.
"What is prosecuted?" said Gavin.'

As it happens Eleanor has picked out Gavin as a promising child, causing feelings of injustice in Honor, who is conscious that only by her lead is Gavin prevented from being at a standstill. The success of Honor's example is demonstrated in the drama of Fulbert's return, when the downfall of Ridley depends on the fact that Gavin has learnt to read writing.

In the schoolroom Eleanor meets with less satisfaction than in the nursery.

' "Mother hasn't a favourite in this room," said Isabel.

... "I don't want to be one of her favoured ones," said Venice, who had a familiar sense of meeting too little esteem.
"She only likes two people in the house, Gavin and Daniel," said Isabel ...
"She likes Father and Luce," said James, just looking up from his book.'

These children belong to the nineteenth-century tradition of such family chronicles as Charlotte M. Yonge's *Daisy Chain* and Juliana Horatia Ewing's *Bad-Tempered Family*, with the significant difference that the author suspends moral judgement. It is the children themselves who judge with ice-cold eyes the antics of the powerful grown-ups. *Parents and Children* could be studied as a text-book on the behaviour of children as they are, and not as theorists feel they should be. The domestic circumstances of the Sullivan children have become as fantastically remote from the world of today as any invented by Mullet the nursery-maid, but the children, in their curiosity and insecurity, are not only contemporary but eternal.

11

EVIL TRIUMPHANT

It has been remarked earlier in this study that crimes per-
petrated by Compton-Burnett characters are not punished by
law. On the other hand transgressors against criminal or
moral codes are not usually undetected by some of their
immediate circle. Anna Donne is an exception. She dominates
Elders and Betters as so perfect a villain that she remains, as
far as the reader can know, completely unexposed and in a
position to enjoy the benefits accruing from her dark deeds.
In *Elders and Betters* even the highlights, the moments of
happiness, are grey, and the shadows, the sins and sorrows,
have the impenetrable blackness of a bog-pool.

At the beginning of the book the Donnes are moving into
a new home, so that Benjamin Donne, father of the family,
may live near his sisters on his retirement from a government
office. Jessica, his eldest sister, is married to Thomas Calderon,
a writer whose success is adequate rather than outstanding,
forcing him to continuous labour to support his own family.
In addition his wife's sister, Sukey, lives under his roof, and
Sukey's inflated idea of her own beauty and charm has always
made her a burden to the Calderons. Now, stricken by mortal
illness, she has become a scourge.

The duenna of the Donne household is a middle-aged
cousin, Clara Bell, who has a fancy to be called Claribel, but
who does not otherwise exert herself in an unonerous

situation. Miss Jennings (Jenney) manages the housekeeping with a good deal of bossy interference from Benjamin's daughter Anna. Jenney is practically the only character in the book with no evil in her composition, and she is one of the principal sufferers from Anna's gruff insensitiveness. Anna excuses her own frequent physical and conversational blunders by insisting that her lapses come from an inability to curb a sincere tongue which speaks from a truthful heart. This heart, it appears later, is open to powerful passions, and closed to pity at any signs of these passions being thwarted. Tumultuous sexual feelings, and deviousness in achieving their satisfaction, bring to mind another plain-faced spinster, Charlotte Mullen, the villain of *The Real Charlotte* by E. OE. Somerville and Martin Ross. Not only did Compton-Burnett express an admiration for this masterpiece of late nineteenth-century fiction, but she went so far as to say that she felt able to identify herself with Charlotte Mullen in Miss Mullen's remorseless pursuit of revenge. Anna Donne is an equally remorseless monster, but her creator did not present her with a need for revenge, perhaps thinking this was a circumstance too horrible to be described.

Before losing his wife Benjamin Donne has also fathered three sons, the two eldest having followed him into the government service in an undisclosed capacity. Bernard, plump and greedy, has a cheerfully philosophical attitude towards his family, but grimness and gloom emanate from Esmond, who tolerates life among his kin solely from reasons of economy. Esmond's grimness resembles the black moods of Clement Gaveston (*A Family and a Fortune*) but, unlike Clement, he seems to have inherited his sour temper from his father.

'[Benjamin] was exasperated by signs of dislike in his sons, and the feeling led him to give them further cause for it.' The youngest son, Reuben, is only thirteen, and petting by

Jenney has been a consolation for a lame leg and the condition
of motherlessness. Ethel, the parlourmaid, and Cook, the
cook, are the only two grown-ups in the household to live in
a comfortable state of reciprocal affection. Ethel's firm explanation for the intensity of their feelings is that they are
first cousins, but her habit of addressing cook as Cook has
given Jenney 'ground for belief that their cousinship was of
recent origin'.

In the garden of the Calderons' house there stands a rock
which is the centre of a religious cult developed by Julius
and Dora, the two youngest of the family. At the ages of
eleven and ten, these children lead rather neglected lives
praying to the god Chung, whom they know, by revelation,
to inhabit the rocky temple, and also offering prayers to the
god of their mother's belief. As their lives include pilfering
to buy forbidden goods, and a reliance on evasions of truth
to escape the consequences, it is suggested that they may feel
'a double share of absolution would not come amiss'. Jessica,
their mother, has a vagueness of mind which at times borders
on melancholia. Her condition is not ameliorated by Thomas,
her husband's, absorption in their daughter Tullia, a situation which the author examines again in later novels. Terence,
the elder son, inclines to a life of minimum exertion, loving
his mother only second to himself, and loved by her without
the qualification. This is the background against which Sukey
is living out the last days of her life, brooding over fancied
neglects from her sister's family, and, convinced that she gets
a poor return for her financial contribution to the household,
indulging in the pleasures of what Samuel Butler called 'will
rattling'. Incidentally, it is difficult to accept, uncritically,
the author's statement that Sukey has an underlying charm
and kindness which wins love, where Jessica might only meet
with affection and esteem.

With practised duplicity the children find no difficulty in

playing off their mother's absentmindedness against the far from strict discipline of Miss Lacy, one of the slacker of Compton-Burnett daily governesses. Miss Lacy is a sedative influence, however, when the two families confront each other, and it becomes clear that Julius and Dora had reason to implore their god Chung that they might be protected from the boldness of the eyes and the lewdness of the tongues of their new relations. By the time the meeting disperses Benjamin has found occasion to speak aside to his son Esmond, muttering that it is of no advantage to his family to be related to a savage. Esmond turns the tables by saying that he, also, is aware of this fact. In addition, Anna has clashed with her aunt Jessica, but the latter is unresentfully relieved to find that Sukey has taken something of a fancy to Anna. It does not enter Jessica's mind that Anna might calculate on a reward for her service. 'Such things did not strike people with regard to Anna.'

The general acceptances of Anna's presentation of herself as a ' "blundering innocent" ' continues to shield her when she embarks on a course neither blundering nor innocent. Sukey accepts her niece as a companion unwearied by too many demands in the past. Anna has the extra motive for haunting the Calderons' house in having fallen in love with her cousin Terence. This passion is so strong that Anna immediately senses danger when Miss Lacy introduces her niece Florence, young and quivering with sexual attraction, into the family circle of her employers. In this mood, Anna makes the most of an opportunity to exchange a few words with Terence on her way to minister to her aunt, though her self-assertion makes the scene a caricature of a flirtation. Anna is then called away by Sukey to help in correcting the wrong done to Jessica and her family in Sukey's latest effort of spiteful 'will-rattling'. Knowing that Jessica has too much integrity to refuse to assist in her own disinheriting, Sukey has worked off her spleen by claiming her sister's help in making a will which leaves all her money to Anna. The old will is still locked in Sukey's desk, and she asks Anna to burn the new one. Sukey is also among those who do not conceive that Anna might expect a return for what she gave. Assured of Anna's compliance, Sukey settles to listen to her niece's reading aloud, sinking first into sleep and then into something deeper. Assuring herself that her aunt can never be disturbed again, Anna substitutes the new will for the old, and openly carries the scroll home, prepared in her mind with a story that she is obeying Sukey's orders, should she be met and questioned. Even when she has burnt the scroll in the fire-place of her own drawing-room she does not relax her pose of someone who has unthinkingly performed a small service for a chair-bound invalid. Anna has coolly taken advantage of an opportunity to do well for herself, and she is unlikely to be troubled by such superstitious feelings as plagued Sophia Stace (*Brothers and Sisters*) after a considerably less calculated exercise in will manipulation.

Anna's precautions are effective. She is alone among Compton-Burnett characters in remembering that 'walls have ears and eyes', so it is with confidence that she can return to the Calderons' house with her father, to lay the foundation for a logical explanation of her coming position as Sukey's heiress. Benjamin and Anna are, of course, met by the news of Sukey's death, and the latter at once mentions that her aunt had been in a disturbed mood, after burning some papers.

With haste that seems to the Donnes slightly indecent, Thomas Calderon opens his sister-in-law's desk, to be faced by the will which leaves all to Anna. Benjamin tells this news, as he supposes it to be, to Anna when his household are assembled at the tea-table. There is a moment of danger for Anna, when, after her repeated, and carefully judged lie that Sukey had, herself, been burning papers, Reuben remarks that he had smelt burning in their own house. Anna had not known her little brother was about, but she replies that a live coal had spurted onto the rug, giving her a shock she could have dispensed with after being with her Aunt Sukey. With unexpected acuteness Reuben points out that Anna had not then known that Sukey was dead, but Anna blocks this awkward ball by saying she recognized her aunt's illness and exhaustion. Anna has a subtle ability to repair her blunders with deftness, while at the same time converting them into evidence to strengthen her own innocence. This skill carries her through some tense moments during a visit from the Calderons. They have come to call with the wildly misconceived idea that Anna will agree that Sukey had intended to burn the new will, so that, in fairness, the money should pass to Jessica and her children. Except for Esmond, whose dislike for his family gives him a truer estimate of Anna's character than others have attained to, the Donne family mass staunchly behind the inheritrix. Anna denies firmly that she had been in Sukey's confidence about the wills, adding with a touch of creative daring that, as she is incapable of invention, any attempt would inevitably lead to her ' "floundering in the mire" '.

Anna is wise to have established this characteristic, because in a moment she is again in danger from her own daring. She makes the mistake of asking for a photograph of Sukey, unaware that her aunt's vanity had caused all old likenesses to be destroyed, and no new ones to be taken. On hearing this, Anna corrects a promise of a photograph to a promise by Sukey that, should her portrait be painted, she would give a photograph of the picture to Anna. Having extricated herself from a tight corner, Anna presses on to make the fact that her family now regret that Sukey's portrait was never painted into yet another brick in the edifice of the Calderon's supposed neglect of Sukey. This operation reinforces Anna's own claims on Sukey's gratitude, while at the same time lessening the Calderons' right to feel disgruntled.

Struggling with her incomprehension at Sukey's change of habit from making a fresh will in a mood of resentment only to destroy it on recovering her temper, Jessica takes Anna into the room where her sister died. The interview is an uneven battle between the volcanic forces concealed under Anna's no-nonsense exterior, and the thin rank of nervous reserves, which is the best Jessica can put into the field. Feeling her way towards an explanation of Sukey's last, apparently unrelenting, action, Jessica is assured by Anna that there could have been no confusion over burning the will, because, Anna says, Sukey's hands were empty and folded in her lap. Not pouncing on a weak point, but merely reflecting her thought, Jessica says that Sukey never folded her hands, but Anna is now growing proficient in covering the slips her rather recent acquaintance with the Calderons causes her to make. She is able to tone down her remark so that Jessica's mind accepts that her niece is telling the truth. However, something stronger than reason, as it might be a telepathic signal from the core of evil in Anna, leads Jessica to take one step further on the road to her own doom.

She appeals to Anna, as a girl without a mother's guidance and living a life with many temptations, not to be afraid to confide in her aunt. Jessica's speech makes it obvious that she knows Anna must have deceived Sukey, but in asking for Anna's confidence she insists, as far as the money is concerned, that Anna can make her own terms, ' ". . . and trust me to keep them. You would not hesitate?"
There was a just perceptible pause.'

If Anna is shocked by her aunt's intuition, or moved by her generosity, it is only for a split second. In the most scorching attack of one character upon another ever written by Compton-Burnett, Anna moves from speaking of her personal fear of the complexities of Jessica's character to a description of the appalling blight cast by her aunt over her family, and over all who come in her path. In her turn Anna's power of telepathic reception warns her that, Jessica being so near the truth, only the harshest onslaught on her aunt's precarious mental balance can protect Anna's own secret. She knows that Jessica's cherishing love will always be a barrier between Anna herself and Terence. She knows, also, that Jessica does not put her own life before the life of one she loves. There has been a revealing scene in the dining-room, when, under the false impression that they are thirteen in number, the assembled company stand hesitating by their chairs, and Jessica, alone, has the courage to risk the threat of an untimely death by sitting down before the others. As the harrowing battle continues, Anna parries her aunt's replies by stigmatising them as the emanations of a diseased mind. Faced by this black picture of herself, Jessica reaches the point of saying that, even it be by a sin, she must free her family from the burden she lays on them, a hint at suicide encouraging for Anna, who would thus be protected for ever from Jessica's suspicions, and free to capture Terence with the lure of her inheritance.

To Terence, when the scene is over, Anna manages to pass a hint that his mother has a double-dealing side to her character, revealed only to Anna herself. To her own family she explains that not only has she been once again assailed by Jessica to give up Sukey's fortune, but that other aspects of Jessica's character, even more deplorable than greed for money, have made themselves only too apparent. In addition Anna uses the barrier which, undeniably, Thomas' devotion to his daughter Tullia has raised between Tullia and her mother, to suggest that Jessica spares men from the burden which her personality lays on women. This mean but skilfully phrased allegation is to counter slight protests from Anna's

father and her brother Bernard that Anna's picture of Jessica
is distorted. Unaware of her criminal ruthlessness, they are
also unaware of her jealousy when faced with beauty and
charm in other women. 'Such things did not strike people
in regard to Anna.'

Soon after Sukey's funeral, Miss Jennings is disturbed by
Ethel, the parlourmaid asking for an interview, in a tone of
voice which gives Jenney the apprehension that separation
from Ethel, and consequently from Cook, may be at hand.
Already wary, Jenney becomes even more nervous when Ethel
goes on to say that the news she has to break is ' "the
worst" '. Ethel is not, however, handing in her notice. ' "The
worst" ' is the news that Tullia, marked out for these shocks,
has found her mother dead, seated in the same armchair in
which Tullia had found her Aunt Sukey so short a time
before. Ethel and Cook have perfected a game of gossip with
Jenney and Bernard, and they cannot allow for any speeding
up of the tempo, so it takes some verbal circumlocution before
they manage to convey that Jessica has killed herself by means
of medicines prescribed for Sukey.

When the news is told to Anna, she at once takes steps to
avert blame from herself for agitating her aunt by a quarrel,
and so precipitating the suicide. Jessica was really making
an attack on Anna, her niece declares, though she adds
that this aspect will be lost to sight in the general distress.
' "There are other aspects of the situation," ' said Esmond.
For Anna, naturally, there are no other aspects. Jessica, the
chief obstacle in the path which leads to Terence has removed
herself, and there is no witness to judge if Anna has been
the propulsive element.

In the Calderons' house, now a house of double mourning,
Anna only pauses long enough to make a few unfortunate
remarks to her uncle before seeking her cousin Terence, alone
and bereft in the library. His father has chosen this moment

to insist that Terence must, in future, exert himself to earn his own living. Terence deplores his father's lack of generosity in being unwilling to share everything with his son, when Thomas can earn a living and Terence cannot. He objects even more at the ungenerosity with which Thomas has said he does not want to support his son's wife and family. Anna takes advantage of the opening offered by Terence's mood, and by his natural wish to talk about his mother. Finally she gives him to understand that Jessica had been so concerned for his future that for him to marry Anna, possessed as she is with Sukey's money, would be a support for her son agreeable to his mother. Terence, selfish but affectionate, is willing to be touched by his mother's concern. Encouraged by this reception of her latest fiction, Anna disposes of the threat of competition from Florence, by adding that Jessica had also talked of Florence, considering her unsuitable for Terence ' "for material and other reasons" '. When Terence says that this remark is not in tone with his mother's speech, Anna assures him that she is not quoting the exact words, not being in the habit of doing so. She feels a natural account is less likely to give an ' "erroneous impression" '.

It would be hard to conceive of an impression more erroneous than the one which Anna has supplied to Terence, but her explanation has fixed matters so that any future slip in her inventions can be written off as a personal paraphrase of conversations with her defunct aunts. She further secures her flank by seating Florence near to Terence, but keeping close enough to monitor their conversation. She has the satisfaction of hearing Florence express the opinion, un- welcome to Terence, that women prefer men to do some work.

Out in the garden, Julius and Dora are praying to the god Chung, their petitions ending, as is their custom, with ' "for Si Lung's sake, amen" ', a formula which they regard as near to 'Son', without advancing to the frontiers of blasphemy. In their prayers they ask to be protected from any hereditary weakness of their mother and aunt, for length of days to compensate for the rigours of childhood and for restraint on their father's part that he may not blight them by talking of their mother but ' "that his heart may know its own bitterness" '. Once again the author uses the bitterness of the heart as an antiphon in the litany of mourning.

When Miss Lacy comes out into the garden over which chill dusk is creeping Dora's composure begins to give way, leading to a passage of gentleness and poetry unique in *Elders and Betters*, and only equalled in emotion by a scene in *Two Worlds and Their Ways*, a novel much less heavy with sinister characterisation.

' "Well, this is not the best time of day for anyone to have to be floating about in the air outside the house," [Dora] said in a jaunty manner.

"No one does have to," said Miss Lacy. "People go into their houses, and spirits have their own safe home."

"Do they really have it?" said Dora, pressing up to her, and using a tone she could not check. "Don't they really have to be about without friends or ease or comfort?" '

Reassurance from Miss Lacy banishes the forlorn moment, and hardly have the children reached their schoolroom than they become locked in combat. Conscious of this lapse in the midst of family grief, they enter it in the book they reserve for their misdemeanours, but they are still able to enjoy the sacrificial incineration of the hair which Julius has torn from Dora's head.

The more ghoulish events of *Elders and Betters* are now over, but their ferment continues to work in the fates of the survivors. Anna's announcement of her engagement to Terence is received by her family with a gasp of incredulity at her readiness to assume the support of a husband so demonstrably work-shy, and, as her father points out, younger than herself. Having reached her goal, Anna is quite prepared to admit that she is buying Terence, and that as he is willing to be bought by her, she is content with a bargain other women might find humiliating.

The scene when the engagement is discussed between the two families is sharpened by a set-to between Tullia (whose character as a doted on and doting daughter becomes progressively more unpleasant as the story advances) and her prospective sister-in-law, Anna. Tullia despises Anna as a plain older cousin, and is not prepared to relinquish her hold on her brother, slight though she admits it to be. Anna has, for her part, taken every opportunity to denigrate Tullia's beauty, and makes it clear that her purchase of Terence will be a complete takeover. Tullia's possessiveness is tried even more highly when Thomas, the father who has dominated her life, announces his engagement to Florence, the niece of Miss Lacy. Fighting against the marriage with a fusillade of patronising ridicule, Tullia is no match for her father's desire for a fresh young mate, a longing which is apt to overtake Compton-Burnett widowers in swift reaction after their bereavement.

Julius and Dora, faced by this manifestation of sexual feelings at different age levels, make an endeavour at comprehension, which enables Tullia to get in a jab at her future stepmother as likely to be a negligible quantity in the household. Tullia has, however, the pleasure of leaving Thomas to cope with the question as to whether Florence will sleep in their father's room. The children accept his assurance that their mother would realise that it would be the right place for his new wife, but Dora reflects that it almost seems a pity that people should look down from heaven. ' "It might prevent them from having perfect bliss." '

This particular obstacle to perfect bliss is, however, soon

to be removed. Bernard takes the opportunity to propose to Tullia, and her acceptance wakes Thomas from his dream of continuing to give his heart to Tullia while enjoying the charms of Florence. It is Florence who actually breaks the engagement, after seeing Tullia and her father locked in an embrace of a closeness that makes it clear that Florence would be superfluous in Thomas's life. Not that Tullia's own engagement is made to be broken, and Florence is quickly re-engaged to Esmond.

This going of the animals into the ark leaves Thomas stranded on the shores of celibacy. With an enthusiasm they find overdone, he turns to his younger children, assuring them that in him they will have a protector and friend as well as a parent. Unhappily, he fails to appreciate the state of sophistication reached by Julius and Dora, and insists that they adopt a mawkish childishness long since outgrown. Bringing this last problem to the temple of the god Chung, they find that their cousin Reuben, previously granted only the position of ' "a sort of servitor" ' is offering a supplication on his own account. Like Julius and Dora, Reuben is faced with a new life of sudden proximity to a father who is almost a stranger. Together the three send up their prayers, imploring protection for the widow and the fatherless, ' "the widower and the motherless" ' being the same thing, as Dora remarks in parenthesis, begging that this protection may save them from this ' "strange travesty" of childhood their father requires from Julius and Dora. After this united act of supplication Dora, in compassion, would be prepared to allow a greater share in companionship to Reuben, but Julius, with a ruthlessness against which he would have appealed to the god Chung had it been visited on himself, refuses to create a precedent. Reuben limps dejectedly away.

Elders and Betters ends on this note of unkindness, almost cruelty. In no other work does Compton-Burnett allow such a consistently low standard of behaviour to prevail among the principal characters. This is particularly to be remarked among the Donnes, where Benjamin has set the tone by installing Claribel as a duenna, but according her no interest or respect. Claribel is able to make her opinion of Benjamin known when there is a discussion on the general rule that widowers remarry. She supposes that to live with a widower who is an exception to this rule has been an experience, 'her voice not implying that it had been a specially absorbing one'.

After the shock of Sukey's death, Anna shows some concern that her father should rest, as a precaution against his own demise. Benjamin has a moment of 'almost incredible gratification that a child of his did not desire his death', lacking the reader's knowledge that Anna might have expedited such an event, unhesitatingly, had it suited her purpose and detection been unlikely. As it is she reaps the benefit of her ill deeds, and the threat of discovery has so far died away that she can discuss herself, a 'blundering innocent', with composure. Terence remarks that is unfair to blame criminals who have been detected by a blunder when others are criminals at heart. Miss Lacy makes a slight criticism that innocence and blundering are not strictly compatible, but those are the sentiments of a bystander. Terence's opinions appear to be ideal for the future husband of Anna.

Throughout *Elders and Betters* the passions of hatred and avarice run so strongly that at times they threaten the suspension of disbelief, vital to the reader's acceptance of any novel. All Compton-Burnett's skill is needed to make it plausible that Terence's regard for Anna's income would lead him so easily to abandon his understanding of his mother, and to accept Anna's version of Jessica's wishes. It has also to be accepted that Anna's brother Esmond, though he has an understanding of Anna's deviousness, is deprived of objectivity by the bitterness of his own frustrated spirit. Consequently he is disabled from deducing that, Anna being the only witness of her dealings with her aunts, her evidence may well be suspect when it contradicts past experience of the habits and reactions of Jessica and Sukey. Leaving Anna victorious, as it might be in an allegorical painting of the Triumph of Evil, her creator turned to scenes in which, though avarice has its influence, hatred is less potent.

12

UPSTAIRS AND DOWNSTAIRS

The claustrophobic atmosphere of *Elders and Betters* is increased by the shabby gentility of its suburban background, shabby gentility of a sort so ably described by Mullet, the nursery-maid in *Parents and Children*. With *Manservant and Maidservant* there is a return to a more spacious establishment, but the gain in dignity brings a loss in comfort, at once to be seen when Horace Lamb and his cousin Mortimer come down to the chilliest of all Compton-Burnett breakfasts. The sullen fire is sending out eddies of smoke, which Bullivant, the butler, and George, his assistant, are summoned to control. A dead jackdaw is extracted from the chimney by the skill of Bullivant, whose gift for dealing with crises, demonstrated throughout the novel, causes Mortimer to like him, George, to dislike and fear him, and Horace, his employer merely to fear him, 'except in his moods of nervous abandonment, when he feared nothing and nobody'. The most uncomfortable manifestation of Horace's nervous composition is a parsimoniousness in domestic matters, by which he ordains that the fire should be lit too late to give a reasonable warmth, and that there should no longer be a choice of tea or coffee at breakfast. The date of the story's opening is established as 1892 by Mortimer Lamb mentioning that he has lived for fifty-four years in the family house, having been born there in 1838. He adds that he is content, which is not strictly true. Although Mortimer does nothing with his time which is not spent in helping Horace run the estate, and although he finds his affection for his cousin an emotional outlet, he has to conceal an even stronger affection for his cousin's wife.

Strong affection is something needed by Charlotte, Horace Lamb's wife. Horace has married her for her money, as she has discovered after marrying him for love. The birth of five children has merely supplied Horace with more victims to stint from any benefit from Charlotte's fortune. Charlotte's love for Horace has gone, but he has still the advantage of her money. She has left until too late any question of remonstrating with her husband about his habit of investing the balance of her income in his own name, Horace believing that to prevent money being spent is the equivalent of earning it. This habit of saving his wife's money causes Horace discomfort, but not enough to make him reduce his miserliness.

In addition to Mortimer, the house also gives a home to Emilia Lamb, a spinster aunt to Mortimer and Horace. A regard for Emelia's seventy-five years has led Bullivant to heap up the fire, which causes Horace to enter into one of his moods of nervous abandonment. He blasts Bullivant for this lavishness with coal, stigmatising it as ' "a great showy pile" '. While Horace is carrying out his principle that penny-pinching is the equivalent of good taste upstairs among his offspring, his wife and Mortimer decide that they must resolve their predicament. When Charlotte returns from a visit to her ageing father, which involves a long voyage, Mortimer insists that they must leave Horace, taking the children with them, before more time of the lives concerned is lost in the misery Horace's behaviour induces. Mortimer feels compunction, perhaps because, as he suggests, Horace may be his own worst enemy, though Charlotte, who suffers for her children as well as herself, does not accept that this is an ' "appealing attribute" '. She points out that those who are their own worst enemies are also bad enemies, if not the worst, to other people.

Belowstairs, Bullivant is supervising the work of his underling George, who has had the humiliation of admitting to the dining-room company that he was born and brought up in the workhouse. Mrs Seldon, the cook, has her own underling Miriam, and it is this quartet who move together through the book, sometimes as participants, sometimes as commentators, in the dramas played by their employers. Miriam, a chubby girl, was found at the age of six months on the steps of the local orphanage, her very name being inherited from a baby who had preceded her there and succumbed. Mrs Seldon is the adherent of an esoteric religious sect, and makes the best of a situation in which Anglicanism is not insisted on. She harries Miriam, but shows some consideration for George, because he is male and not Miriam. The same principle operates in reverse with Bullivant, to whom Miriam has the merit of being female and not being George. In addition Bullivant, one of the author's most genial butlers, has roguish tendencies, which he can even display when lending his voice to support Mrs Seldon in the hymns of her cult. Though it has its pains, this life belowstairs, in the orbit of the kitchen fire with cups of tea continually brewing, compares favourably with the arctic schoolroom, where Horace and Charlotte's children are growing up in spiritual and physical discomfort. A peremptory ring, in the style of Mullet's father (*Parents and Children*), may summon Bullivant at any hour, but the kitchen is safe from an angry invasion by Horace, against which his children have no defence.

Nipped by the chill of their father's avarice, the five little Lambs are drawn almost in monochrome, compared with the portraits in strong colours which make the young Sullivans in *Parents and Children* so memorable. This technique is well suited to their pinched and ragged condition. They first appear when their father bursts in on them to complain about the outrageous size of yet another fire, venting the worst of his ill-will on Sarah, aged thirteen and his eldest child, an unenviable position in that she is the buffer that protects the younger children from their father's wrath. Her reward is the love they give her as the softener of life's hardships. With an awkward squad at his command, Horace drills Sarah, Jasper, Marcus and Tasmin who descend in age in yearly steps, as well as Avery, the seven-year-old baby of the family, until they are wise enough to admit that they are warm. Horace's fulminations on the subject of the over-filled fire-place at length reduce his son Marcus to tears, the point to which Horace always carries an argument, considering that to achieve victory his opponent should weep, so he has 'no experience of defeat in words'.

Charlotte arrives in the schoolroom, bringing such kindness and comfort with her, that at tea-time Jasper feels brave enough to ask his father for some ' "stalecake" ', pronounced in one word, 'as staleness was a condition of their having it'. Even Avery has remarked that when Horace has been particularly cross he will sometimes give things to his children, but on this occasion Horace spoils the effect of his meagre generosity by returning to the schoolroom with further strictures on the behaviour of the long-suffering Sarah. He announces, also, that the education of the four eldest, hitherto frugally conducted by their great-aunt Emilia, is now to be undertaken by a tutor. Horace departed, Marcus moulds a wax candle into the image of a man, with helpful hints from the others which make it recognisably a statuette of their father.

' "Put pins round the head," said Jasper . . .

"Not quite so many pins," said Avery.'

Appositely a message comes to ask the children's nurse for some lotion. Horace, at a change of the wind, has had a return of rheumatism. At the brilliant success of Marcus's magic, Avery, softhearted and less consistently exposed to Horace's bullying, shows signs of going into a screaming fit, so that the candle has to be thrown on to the fire to placate him. However, Marcus points out that the candle has not been wasted, having had ' "a noble history and a martyr's end" '.

Horace does not have a noble history for the rest of the day, martyred though he feels himself to be at dinner by the addition of an extra cutlet to the number he considers adequate. Also he has to listen to the unpleasant news that his wife has altered her will, so that her children and Mortimer will have a share in her estate. In this mood it is a release for Horace to discover George, the footman, helping himself to the pudding it is his duty to return to the kitchen. George is told that his behaviour must prevent him from achieving a grown man's wages in the foreseeable future, but the family is still at the dinner table when there is a further commotion outside the dining-room door. George is discovered in the act of shaking Avery, who has made a raid on a box of comfits (sweets to a later generation), which is kept in a nearby cupboard. Subsequent recriminations from Horace, who learns that another of his sons, Jasper, has also the habit of pilfering, brings Avery to such a condition of collapse that he has to be comforted with some of the sweets he had been attempting to steal.

In this bleak atmosphere, Charlotte travelling to a far continent, Emilia and Mortimer doubtful protection from their father, the children face Gideon Doubleday, their new tutor. Gideon himself finds it hard to keep his eyes from the ragged clothes of his pupils, particularly the boys' sailor suits which are not only too juvenile for their ages but out of elbows as well. In a cross-examination of the tutor, the children discover that Gideon has made the mistake of ordering five French reading books, under the optimistic illusion that Horace will be willing to pay for the copy that Gideon proposes to retain for his own use. Mr Doubleday has not learnt the lesson promulgated by Edith Hallam (*Daughters and Sons*) that asking for new books is resented by private employers more than many ' "graver things" '. The cross-examination takes in the question of the tutor's salary, and, though Gideon tries to disguise that Horace had attempted to reduce the standard rate, he is aware that Sarah, at least, is not deceived. Horace arrives to cast an eye over the educational progress, and by mentioning the fire causes Gideon to rise and put on more coal.

' "Mr. Doubleday's time is money in more than one sense," murmured Tasmin.'

Another cross-examination awaits Gideon at home, where his mother, Gertrude, and his unmarried sister, Magdalen, are anxious to hear all details of the cheese-paring that constricts the life of Gideon's new pupils. If Gertrude Doubleday is among the more strangling of Compton-Burnett mothers, she is dealt with by mockery that is almost kindly. Supposed to bear a likeness to George Eliot, Gertrude fancies the idea sufficiently to keep a portrait of this author on her wall, 'though she was aware that [George Eliot's] physiognomy was not her strong point, and had no misgivings about her own . . .'. Her daughter's eye has been caught by Mortimer's attractive personality, and Gertrude is anxious to meet Horace Lamb during his grass-widowerhood. Gideon is surprised at his mother urging that an invitation should be sent to the Lambs, being unaware that his mother relishes a meeting with any man within twenty years of her own age, and is prepared to stretch the age-limit.

At the tea-party thus arranged it is Horace who remarks on his hostess's likeness to the picture of George Eliot, but it is Mortimer who notices that Gertrude has emphasized this chance resemblance by copying the dress of her famous counterpart. Excited by these new acquaintances, Gertrude asks the entire Lamb family, a party of eight, to luncheon on Christmas Day, but Emilia, although unable to control Horace's domestic practices, is sufficiently agile, socially, to reverse the invitation. In their all-knowingness, Bullivant and Mrs Seldon have already foreseen that there will be three extra for luncheon at Christmas, so that Bullivant accepts the news without a quiver of surprise when the Lambs return home. The journey has been made on foot, but this action, seen as unpretentious by Gertrude, shocks Bullivant on account of Emilia's seventy-five years. Horace defends himself from criticism, unspoken but hanging in the frosty air, by saying that the horses are valuable beasts who should be protected from the cold, valuing a pair of horses above one single aunt.

It is no surprise to find that Christmas Day is conducted on an equally chilly note, Horace seizing the opportunity of his wife's absence to dock the Christmas stockings of the four elder children. After this uncheerful festival has passed, Miss Buchanan makes her appearance in the story, a woman who conceals the handicap of illiteracy. She has organised her grocery shop with such skill that she has no need to read the labels on the goods, but her real peril of exposure comes from a notice that says letters may be delivered and collected from this address. Miss Buchanan's surly demeanour adds to the unease of those who avail themselves of this method of keeping their correspondence secret. Gertrude Doubleday is among the surreptitious customers of Miss Buchanan. Having insisted that all letters in her own household should be general property she is obliged to use subterfuge to conceal an innocuous correspondence with relations too lowly for 'her open recognition'.

Undeterred by Miss Buchanan's guarded behaviour, Mrs Doubleday can smell that something is concealed, and presses the question as to what reading matter occupies the shopkeeper's leisure, adding a threat of books to be lent and their contents to be discussed. Additionally, Gertrude disrupts Miss Buchanan's system for dealing with the letters delivered to her address. The system's success depends on the postman reading the name of the addressee, Miss Buchanan, with truth, declaring that she finds handwriting difficult. At the door of the shop, Gertrude claims a letter from the postman as her own, later seeing that it is not, and asking her daughter, who has come to meet her, to return the letter to Miss Buchanan. At some distance from her mother, Magdalen sees to whom the letter is addressed, and palms it in her glove for her own purposes.

These purposes are revealed in an outbreak of hysteria from Magdalen at the family luncheon table. Gertrude has not been daunted in her pursuit of Horace Lamb by the obvious uneasiness displayed by his family at table on Christmas Day. It is this concentration of feeling on Horace that causes Magdalen to accuse her mother of engineering a situation in which Mortimer, isolated, is being driven to plan the break-up of the home. Exhilarated rather than affronted by this attack, which she finds flattering in its implication that she exudes sexual attraction, Gertrude condoles with her daughter on a jealousy rooted in Magdalen's spinsterhood. With an equal gusto she uses the familiar phrase ' "breakers ahead" ' to predict the future to Gideon should Mortimer fail to respond to Magdalen. Gideon says, rather plaintively, that if all his professional engagements reached this sort of climax he might be forced into premature retirement.

Riding the breakers together, Gertrude and Magdalen set

off for Mr Lamb's house, Gertrude seeing that her daughter's unexpectedly intimate knowledge of an impending domestic explosion gives an opportunity to make closer friends with Horace. After the two visitors have left, Emilia tells Horace of Magdalen's infatuation for Mortimer, handing Horace a letter which seems to have fallen to the ground. Horace is convalescent from a chill, and Emilia assumes that a restless, disturbed state, in which she finds him later in the day, is due to the idea that Mortimer may be leaving him, working on Horace's weakened condition.

The revolution that now takes place is not the one that has been expected. Charlotte returns, unheralded, to be puzzled both by an atmosphere of greater comfort in the home and a happier companionship between Horace and the children. Mortimer, on the other hand, seems to be cut off from the unity with his cousin, never previously impaired by his feelings for Charlotte. Horace is almost smugly conscious of his own efforts at reformation, taking pleasure in analysing the unhappy past, and putting no check on his children's criticisms. Totally confused by developments, Mortimer and Charlotte agree, at length, that the home is now a happy one and that their hopes of a life together had been based on its unhappiness, though they are still baffled as to how Horace, not given to speculation, can have found out their plans to take his family from him. This is still not revealed when the show-down with Horace takes place, and Charlotte speaks powerfully of the crushing of her young children by their father, which will leave its mark on them for their lives. Between Horace and Mortimer there is an even more wonderful scene, lacking the pain which makes Dudley Gaveston's denunciation of his brother Edgar (A *Family and a Fortune*) so moving, but touchingly comic as Mortimer listens with horrified despair to the plans by which Horace designs to neutralise his cousin.

Mortimer does not deny that it is necessary for him to leave the home of all his life, but now that Charlotte will no longer leave with him, how, he asks Horace, can he live? With what Mortimer calls a use of power with ' "moderation and cruelty" ', Horace tells his cousin that he may remain in the neighbourhood if he marries. ' ". . . [Magdalen Doubleday] would give you all she has. Her heart is in her eyes when she looks at you." ' Even in this tight corner, Mortimer is irrepressible. ' ". . . My heart is in my mouth when you talk of it. Perhaps it does sound as if we might have something in common. . . ." '

With Magdalen for a wife, Horace proposes to settle Mortimer in a cottage beside a mill on the estate. Mortimer says that it would certainly be a damp enough place in which to face death, the living death to which Horace is condemning him. In these exchanges, the reader should not be mesmerised by the neatness of the dialogue. Every sentence pushes the story forward, as Horace sanctimoniously exiles his cousin to a loveless marriage in a damp cottage and Mortimer refuses to accept his fate with resignation.

' "How many more meals shall I eat in my old home?"

"Not many more," said Horace.

"I somehow do not think things will taste the same in the house by the mill. Have you thought about my appetite there? Or am I really going there to face death?" '

The cottage by the mill also gets a bad character from Gertrude when she is faced by the news that it is to be her daughter's married home. Anyone less determined would have abandoned her efforts to corral Horace on the return of Charlotte, but Gertrude makes a last effort, simultaneously attempting to keep Magdalen and Mortimer apart. Failing in both endeavours, Gertrude storms out, venting her feelings by a diatribe against the cottage by the mill, which even the better class of working people have left in search of a different situation.

Gertrude's ruffled feelings become calmer on the way home, besides taking more kindly to her daughter's prospects, she experiences some relief that her own future will be undisturbed, a sensation that has occurred to other characters in the earlier novels. After a moment's chagrin, Sir Godfrey Haslam accepts complacently that the terms of his wife's will prevents him from marrying Camilla (*Men and Wives*). Josephine Napier rejoices almost openly that she can return to the school which is her creation, after a brief dream of marrying Felix Bacon and joining the baronetage (*More Women than Men*). Even the spinster cousins in *A House and Its Head*, each jealous of the other as the stung are of the adder in their pursuit of the Vicar, are, in the end, ready to be glad that he chooses neither for his wife. This is not the last time that Compton-Burnett demonstrated her belief that the comforting grip of the familiar can be stronger than stirrings of a desire for the changes marriage would bring.

To return to Mortimer and his engagement to Magdalen, it is Emilia who supplies what little balm she can by leaving him to have a chat with Bullivant, a relaxation habitual and soothing to both of them. Bullivant agrees that his mind boggles at the picture of Mortimer in the execrated cottage by the mill, though he questions Horace's wish that Mortimer should keep away from his former home. Bullivant considers he knows Horace's mind better than its owner, and he guardedly admits that he knows what has precipitated this unhappy banishment for Mortimer. In the kitchen, in conversation with Mrs Selden, Bullivant presents a gloomy view and Mrs Selden suggests that Mortimer's engagement, should, at present, be concealed from George, already in trouble for words considered to be blasphemous.

Mortimer has chosen marriage because it will, at least, allow him to remain in the neighbourhood, if only in a little damp house, reminiscent of the one inhabited by Beatrix Potter's Jeremy Fisher. He is deprived of even this foothold in his former world by a sudden revelation of Magdalen's real nature, previously concealed under a carefully gentle manner. Going to inquire at Miss Buchanan's shop for a letter from Charlotte never received by him, Mortimer meets his fiancée and her mother. It becomes clear that the missing letter was taken in error by Gertrude, handed by her to Magdalen, but never returned to Miss Buchanan. Pressed by Mortimer as to why she had read the letter, in what he says was a rather premature observation of the customs of married life, Magdalen says that they could hardly begin these habits too soon. Mortimer replies that he now understands that his fiancée has acted on principle, having earlier judged her by himself and assumed that she has unsuccessfully resisted temptation. (In a philosophical aside Mortimer wonders how those who successfully resist temptation can be known to have been tempted.) Continuing with his cross-examination of Magdalen, Mortimer extracts the information that she cannot return the letter to him. As her evil deeds are on a petty scale compared to the doings of Sybil Edgeworth or Anna Donne, Magdalen is more easily brought to confess the whole truth, that the letter was dropped on ' "the floor of a room" '. Mortimer at last understands the source of Horace's information, which has been used with such a shattering effect, and though Magdalen struggles to maintain the engagement, Mortimer retreats from it inexorably.

' "A quick release is the merciful thing . . . And neither of us will live in the house by the mill. The cloud is a dark one, but it has its silver lining." '

Bullivant is now applied to by Mortimer to find an economical lodging, which is, in theory to be Mortimer's place of permanent exile, but, while agreeing to keep up this pretence, Bullivant's omniscience allows him to hint that he takes a less gloomy view. Agreeing also to Mortimer's admonition to have a care for Horace, Bullivant says that he may be able, by skilled insinuation, to let his master know that this had been Mortimer's final thought.

The focus of the story shifts with the departure of Mortimer, dramas in the kitchen and the nursery taking the place of romantic crises in the lives of parents and employers. Mortimer has instigated one of these dramas, before his departure. He has deduced that Miss Buchanan's curious business habits conceal illiteracy, and, confiding this secret to Bullivant, suggests that Miss Buchanan's isolation might be eased by an invitation from the kitchen party. Assuring Mortimer that a woman's secret will be safe with him, Bullivant follows the kindly suggestion and Miss Buchanan comes to tea. The party can be counted as a success, although Miss Buchanan's secret is at moments in peril, from such threats as labels on jam-pots or texts on Mrs Seldon's pious tea-cups. Bullivant himself, riled by Miss Buchanan's inadvertent laughter at a joke of George's mocking the butler, lays a trap for the guest with a wine list, but she side-steps with practised skill. The chapter ends with a sparring match between Cook and Bullivant, in which the former convinces the latter that she knows Miss Buchanan's secret, which is then revealed to her. Cook challenges Bullivant on his attempt to confound Miss Buchanan by asking her to read the wine list, and having accepted his explanation that the ' "vein of impishness" ' has been his bane, confesses that she herself has claimed to know of Miss Buchanan's disability to lure Bullivant to let out the secret. With this glimpse into the darker side of each other's characters honours between these two heads of domestic departments may be said to be even.

Five weeks have gone by since Mortimer's departure, and upstairs in the dining-room Horace is showing ominous signs of relapse into old abhorred habits of fault-finding. The new custom of the children appearing at breakfast has caused Charlotte misgivings from 'the threat of the hour', fears shown to be justified when one of the boys identifies an unopened letter as being addressed to Horace in Mortimer's handwriting. A stiff lecture from Horace on the sacredness of other people's correspondence follows, given with no less conviction because the speaker has taken every advantage of a letter to another placed in his way. Mortimer's letter, when Horace comes to read it, is nicely calculated to throw him off his balance, with reference to a prohibition from Horace against Mortimer writing to him and an assurance that Mortimer would never be so malicious as to take Horace at his word. Horace's letter has, of course, broken Mortimer's heart. Emilia has the courage to ask what Mortimer has to say, and receives a snubbing reply from Horace, but Charlotte comes to the aunt's support by pointing out that Horace cannot spend the next thirty years denying his own nature and the feelings of his heart.

With these feelings much disturbed, Horace goes for a walk, saying a kind word to Jasper and Marcus, as he passes them at work in the garden. His sons watch him as he walks out of earshot and admit to each other that Horace is going towards a bridge which spans a ravine, a bridge they know to be unsafe, though sound in appearance. Horace, the boys also know, is ignorant of the peril connected with features of the landscape unusually dramatic in a Compton-Burnett countryside.

Marcus and Jasper work it out that their will to warn Horace had been weakened by the threat, at that morning's breakfast, that bullying and tyranny might be reviving. Hysterics at the probability of guilt for the death of a father, recently become kind, are heard by Charlotte, and steps are taken to prepare for Horace's return dead, moribund or at least on a stretcher. Actually he reappears uninjured, having found the bridge blocked by a warning notice. Congratulation and relief, however, give way to horror on Horace's part, when he discovers that his sons had watched him going to possible death, with inertia brought on by the fear that the bad old times might be returning. Like other Compton-Burnett tyrants, Horace holds the view that his own failings are to be excused to one weighed down by the burden of family cares, but bad reaction to these failings by others is inexcusable as they do not carry his burdens. In this mood he is asking rhetorically what is to be done when an offer of help comes in the welcome though unexpected voice of Mortimer. His return cools the exaggerated heat that Horace has been building up round Marcus and Jasper and their unhappy lapse. Horace, taken unaware, greets Mortimer with affectionate enthusiasm, and then finds it difficult to back-pedal. Mortimer, having the advantage of knowing of Horace's own lapse, uses it with witty skilfulness. He has returned, he says, because he has heard Horace's voice calling his name. When Horace supposes that this is a visit of a few hours, Mortimer says that Horace knows he is not speaking the truth. Horace asks about luggage, but any reassurance he might get from hearing that Mortimer has brought very little, is cancelled by learning that Bullivant ' "has only packed things for a few weeks" '.

Having shown Horace the forces that are massed in favour of an amnesty, Mortimer points out that if he had not betrayed his cousin, Horace, in his turn, could not have betrayed Mortimer by reading the letter from Charlotte, which has caused Horace to amend his harsh ways and win the hearts of his children. In a feeble attempt to parry Mortimer's counter-attack, Horace asks;
' "What letter?"
"Horace, this is unworthy of you." '

128

Like a chess player sacrificing minor pieces for ultimate advantage, Mortimer allows Horace to know that his love for Charlotte has weakened; he even gives up his effort to retain the increase in his allowance which has supported him in his exile. Honour and parsimony alike satisfied, Horace gratefully accepts Mortimer back into his home, and turns his attention to reproving Marcus and Jasper for their patricidal tendencies. The gap between his sons and himself remains as deep as the gulf down which he is obstinately convinced that they wished him to fall. Only the boys show sense in this predicament by refusing to join their father in a penitential pilgrimage to the bridge of ill-omen.

The drama of the day is only beginning. Sharp-eared as a hare for the sound of any assault on domestic supplies, Horace, during luncheon, detects George in the act of helping himself to goods from the cupboard in which the seldom-used luxuries of the household are stored, eatables that George has been in the habit of taking to his friends on his free afternoons. Asked by Horace what he should say if required to give George a character, George, in unhelpful desperation, can only suggest that a character for Horace's own sons would present a worse problem. Bullivant hustles George out of the room, with Horace's command that George should appear before him on returning from his outing in which he will, presumably, bestow the stolen goods on his friends. Horace is unaware that George has made an instant resolution to cast himself into the ravine, already the cause of a family upset, rather than face his master's judgement on his pilfering habits.

By way of winding up his resolution to this exit, designed to be a revelation of noble depths in George's character unsuspected by Horace, George pauses at Miss Buchanan's shop to indulge himself for the last time with sweets and tobacco. The Doubleday family are also in the shop, and Gertrude remarks on the niceness of ' "the young footman" '. She has drawn George into conversation by admiring his pocket knife, an object vaguely familiar to Gideon the tutor. At the news of Mortimer's return, Gertrude insists that she will pay a call that afternoon, her appetite for crashing in on a delicate situation being whetted by Gideon's account of increased tensions in his employer's home.

George, in the meantime, speeds up the hill, realising that its steepness indicates the depth into which he plans to cast himself. 'His breathing quickened, impeded, as it was, by exertion and the consumption of the sweetmeat. Waste was not to be feature of George's last hour. . . .' George's personality has always tended to get out of hand, and he now works himself up to a belief that his plan of suicide, preceded by removing the warning notice and leaving a note to say that the bridge was still unsafe, will be a lesson that Horace will receive with ' "remorse and gratitude" '.

Unfortunately, it becomes apparent that George's mood of exaltation has evaporated with only the initial stage of his plan carried out. Horace returns from the bridge in an acute condition of 'nervous abandonment', having remarked the displaced notice board as he was on the point of crossing over. Horror on horror, he has also found a knife, given by him to Marcus for Christmas. Refusing to accept the explanation that the knife has been lost for months, Horace adopts an almost gloating note as he lays before the assembled family the incontrovertible evidence that, this time, his sons' intentions have been actively, rather than passively, patricidal. Sarah's word that she knows the knife to have been lost, a loss concealed from her father because he makes a crime of an accident, is also swept aside. Whether the nurse's protest, that she knows the boys to be incapable of such thought-out villainy, would have led Horace to give up his determination to be a victim will never be known. Bullivant, anxious to be present at the scene, announces Gertrude and Gideon Doubleday, replying to an inquiry, made aside by Mortimer, that any interruption would be beneficial. Bullivant is right, for Gideon at once recognises the knife, that is the main evidence against Marcus and Jasper, as the knife that George has displayed, earlier, in Miss Buchanan's shop. Mrs Doubleday, with a weakness for George, attempts to contradict Gideon by suggesting a duplicate knife, but, luckily for the boys, Gideon is too sure of his facts to be shaken. Gertrude's gift for volte-face is one of her more endearing qualities, and she at once reminds the company that, on seeing their trouble, she had prophesised a swift return of happiness. Having thus taken to herself the merit for the family's shift to tears of affection and words of gratitude, Gertrude then proceeds to put in an appeal that George may be dealt with sympathetically, asking also that he may be told that Mrs Doubleday had spoken on his behalf, in the conviction that his behaviour can be explained by some trial of ' "health or nerves or personal situation" '.

'There was silence, while people faced the demand, which in Horace's case seemed considerable.'

It is to Bullivant that the task falls of bringing George's infamy home to him, and pointing the way of repentance, an opportunity for the full use of the butler's histrionic talents, assisted, as he is, by the force of Cook's religious fervour. George bluffs desperately, but at length he is brought to admit everything, except that his nerve failed when faced with the prospect of killing himself to escape having to face an interview with Horace. This left him no alternative but to sacrifice his master. Miss Buchanan joins the party in time to witness George embracing Bullivant's knees in an agony of remorseful fear. To Miss Buchanan, an outsider, Bullivant's hyperbolical injunction that George should fix his gaze on ' "a pure and unsullied future" ' is only too obviously a threat

131

to her composure. Reacting swiftly to the visitor's suppressed laughter, the butler suggests that she should lead the thoughts of the company to better things by reading a passage from the Bible. This counter-attack is observed by Cook who, in her own good time, casts a dart of reproof obliquely at her colleague.

George remains in abeyance, as Bullivant puts it, so he is not present in the dining-room when, Horace having had a bad relapse into parsimony, Mortimer piles up the fire as an act of ' "a brave man and a gentleman" '. On this occasion Horace is in no position to display rage, his economy of fuel in the bitter cold having precipitated one of those attacks of pneumonia which bring Compton-Burnett characters to the door of eternity, and sometimes over the threshold. Lying between life and death, Horace insists that his five children should be brought to his bedside, and, for once secure from the risk of deflating replies, speaks to each of the way he has never learnt to gain their love. Having fulfilled this duty, Horace sinks into a sleep that might be deathly, and though Charlotte and Mortimer view the situation with pain and pity, it is in the kitchen that material as well as spiritual aspects are considered.

Although sincerely attached to Horace, Bullivant has already plotted the details of the funeral etiquette. Cook has an adequate supply of black garments on which to draw for the occasion, and Bullivant has a surplus to hand that will enable him to clothe George as well as himself. As it happens the obsequies which would necessitate this mustering of sable apparel are indefinitely postponed. The dining-room bell, thought to be the passing bell for Horace, turns out to be rung to announce that he has taken a turn towards recovery. But even when convalesence advances the group in the kitchen are reluctant to abandon speculation on the chair that might have been empty, and on Mortimer's potential as a father to the children, speculations stimulated by the presence of Miss Buchanan. George has returned to his state of smouldering revolt, and chooses this occasion to lay bare Miss Buchanan's secret, which he has learnt from eaves-dropping. Bullivant is, however, in no position to reprove his underling as his past impish teasing of Miss Buchanan is now made plain to the victim herself. Unexpectedly, the revelation of her handicap leads to Miss Buchanan's escape from its shadow. Miriam, the kitchen-maid, has suffered throughout the book from snubs delivered by Cook, and a lack of fellow-feeling from George, who considers her slow and slave-minded. She now comes into her own, for her gentle patience has been found suitable to teach backward children in her orphanage. The upper-servants agree that, with suitable safeguards to prevent Miriam from acquiring self-importance, Miss Buchanan, large, pale, ponderous and fifty-eight, shall come to the kitchen to be given reading lessons by Miriam, red-faced, roundabout and sixteen years old.

From this scene of constructive friendliness Bullivant is summoned by Horace's premptory ring, to end the book as it started by a command to deal with a smoking fire. The butler attributes the burst of smoke to a vagary of the wind, and when Horace suggests that the wind must be a woman, Bullivant takes the last trick by pointing out that he knows from his profession this is a frequent thing to be. To the butler's further remark that one would not wish to speak against this fact, Horace maintains a silence that seems un-likely to be that of consent.

After a preponderance of evil-feeling, charmless characters in *Elders and Betters*, it is a relief to have had to do with a less depressing set in *Manservant and Maidservant*. It is as if the author has turned a corner in a dark tunnel, and emerged into a brighter landscape. Among the dependent bachelors who supply so much of the *raisonneur* element in

Compton-Burnett novels none has more charm and more wit than Mortimer Lamb. With the exception of Deakin, the butler in *A Heritage and Its History*, no servant gives more philosophical loyalty to his employer's fortunes than Bullivant. Mortimer and Bullivant spin a cocoon of affection round Horace, protecting him from the worst effects of his mishandling of his children. Between themselves, they discuss the mystery of the feeling which attaches them both to Horace, knowing nothing of its essence except that they share it. This loving of the apparently unlovable is a theme to which the author recurs repeatedly throughout her novels. Her characters fall out of love with the objects of their sexual passions, to return with thankfulness to situations and persons, often demonstrably intolerable, but having the redeeming feature that the worst is known.

13

BACK TO SCHOOL

The main crisis in *Two Worlds and Their Ways* is precipitated by too much maternal love, rather than by too little paternal affection, the cause of so much trouble in *Manservant and Maidservant*. Sir Roderick and Lady Shelley are the over-doting parents of Clemency and Sefton, their mother's passion that her children should be successful being complicated by her own unease as a second wife. The first Lady Shelley has left a son, Oliver, whose presence in the house is a permanent reminder to Maria, his stepmother, that her own son is blocked from the rights of succession. Maria, a woman who strives for virtue, has achieved a friendly relationship with Oliver, which covers Mr Firebrace, Oliver's grandfather and another resident legacy from Sir Roderick's first wife. Sir Roderick himself is a particularly ramshackle and poverty haunted baronet, with a habit of calling his wife ' "my pretty" ', impressive to his hearers by the endearment's grotesque inappropriateness. In a passage that rises into poetry, the reader is told that to Sir Roderick's vivid blue eyes the most 'satisfying vision was the flat green land about his fading walls, and his only music the wind in his native trees sighing over the ground where he would lie. To be without it would to be without a grave.'

The fading walls also shelter a governess, Miss Petticott (called Petticoat by the children in joke, and by Sir Roderick in aberration) Adela, once the nurse and still the comforter, and Aldom the butler, a monkey of a man with eyes as blue as Sir Roderick's. It is Adela and Aldom who provide relief for the children from the oppression caused by their parent's over-anxious concern with character building and education. Aldom provides more than this, as he has an uncontrollable histrionic gift, displayed in the schoolroom, where Miss Petticott by her careful absence permits what she knows she cannot prevent.

A Hardyesque scene in which Aldom acts out the drama of fetching his father from a supper at the local inn, is interrupted by a visit from Maria to the schoolroom. Although Adela has requested Aldom to censor his language, the butler, alert for his mistress's approach, runs no risk, and turns his performance into that of a village schoolmaster. Maria has a vague disquiet about the ubiquity of Aldom in her children's lives, but the cover-up habits tacitly shared by those concerned, including Miss Petticott and Adela, produce a plausible explanation for any situation Maria surprises. Aldom's performance, Maria is assured, comes from a rumour that the children may be going away to school. Their parents have, in fact, been approached on this subject by the sisters of Sir Roderick's first wife, Lesbia Firebrace, principal of a girl's school, and Juliet, married to Lucius Cassidy, who runs a preparatory school for boys.

There is a supposition that these ' "governesses" ', as Mr Firebrace classifies those of his family engaged in education, may actually be touting for pupils, and their arrival to discuss the matter does not entirely dispel the idea. Lesbia, whatever her motives, has no doubt that Clemence should go to the school over which Lesbia herself presides. On the other hand, Lucius considers that his preference for his own educational methods disqualifies him from recommending his own establishment. His wife Juliet, whose comments are always sharp and often scandalous, suggests that Julius's attitude contributes to the school's prosperity, people seeming to prefer that their sons should go where they are not wanted. Immediately the question of the children going to school appears to be settled, Lesbia begins to take the line that she may have no vacancy for Clemence, being a believer in keeping parents properly suppliant. To the discussion a ' "sensitive and subdued accompaniment" ' on the piano is contributed by Oliver, with sufficient skill for Lucius to make yet another 'governess' in the family by engaging Oliver as his music master.

Still debating the comparative value of a school or a home education, the parents and Lesbia visit the schoolroom to find the children, Miss Petticott, and Adela, sitting enthralled before a figure whose grey fringe of horse-hair snatched from Adela's armchair recalls another scene of mimicry, Chilton's impersonation of Sabine, his grandmother in *Daughters and Sons*. Although Aldom has only added a scarf and a cloak to his usual clothes, his mimicry is a sufficiently accurate take-off of Lesbia, for its object to remark that if Clemence is not prepared for her new life it is through no fault of Aldom's.

The imminence of their departure for school shows their father, but not their mother, where in their home Clemence and Sefton have fixed their hearts. Sefton comes downstairs on the pretext of looking for a book, an imaginary work, on the subject of thinking that someone at a distance might be ill would have the power to make them so. Perhaps not unnaturally, Maria takes this anxiety as applying to herself, and sends Sefton reassured up to bed. Sir Roderick, following to say good-night to his children, overhears Sefton's passionate avowal to Adela that he suffers agonies in the night from thinking that his nurse might be ill or dead, Clemence agreeing that she has scarcely outgrown this terror. The emotion of this scene has been compared earlier to Dora

Calderon's moment of self-revelation to Miss Lacy the governess after Dora's mother's suicide (*Elders and Betters*). Adela's method of comfort is to gather the children into her armchair and croon consolation over them, a less intellectual approach than Miss Lacy's but equally efficacious. Sir Roderick does not interrupt the scene, and when Maria gives Adela a patronisingly good character, adding smugly that it has been seen to whom Sefton turns in his real need, her husband agrees that this has been demonstrated, 'perhaps feeling that he had a right to say this'.

Lesbia Firebrace as a headmistress is less overwhelming in her domination than Josephine Napier (*More Women than Men*), and her teaching staff are, inappropriately, less actively lesbian than Josephine's. The two headmistresses share, however, the faculty of seeming to be absent from a scene while remaining within earshot, a characteristic emulated by some of the staff. ' "This place is a nest of professional eavesdroppers," ' remarks Esther, the toughest of Clemence's form mates. She has just been overheard by her headmistress speculating on whether the school is deteriorating, and again by her form mistress as she relates her father's complaints about her school bills. The words 'professional eavesdroppers' are at once justified by Leslia's reappearance, with a stiff comment that only Esther's habit of saying things she wishes unheard leads her to fear eavesdropping. It is Esther who leads the inquisition into Clemence's circumstances, and traps the poor new girl into a series of pathetic evasions. The style of Clemence's home and the position of her father are so at variance with her out-of-date wardrobe, and the shabby appearance of her mother, that she is driven to invent clothes left at home, and to demote her mother to the position of an attendant governess. The bullying increases both Clemence's uncertainty in her new life and her wish to do well in it. Her gifts are good, but not adequate to keep her always in the highest place, so she begins to follow a course of cheating, which is first suspected by her form mates, and then revealed during an examination. Clemence has allowed the wish to please her parents by her success to blind her from imagining the results of being detected in her cheating. She faces the Christmas holidays with the time-bomb of her school report ticking ever nearer to its explosion.

In the meantime Sefton has arrived at Lucius Cassidy's school, in the company of his half-brother Oliver. Sefton is soon brought to tears by his schoolmates, who, learning that this new boy's mother is a second wife, insist that she must be a concubine. Miss James the matron, a rock of kindness in the cruel ocean of school life, before tending another new boy, Sturgeon, who has vomited some potted meat, corrects this outrageous suggestion.

A grown-up version of the going-over given to Sefton is taking place in the masters' common-room, with Oliver Shelley as its object. Julia Cassidy, from a sniping post that she occupies as wife of the headmaster, has already remarked that an instant sympathy has developed between Oliver and Spode, a master who has arrived at the same moment. They have also, Julia says, a resemblance to each other. (This likeness is a clue to a secret, as is the likeness of Aldom's blue eyes to Sir Roderick's.) Spode has explained to Oliver that he teaches because his mother prefers to spend her inheritance from her own father on fox-hunting, rather than to give her son an adequate allowance. Spode explains, also, that his vivid imagination has prevented him from hunting and so gaining his grandfather's esteem and a legacy for himself. Oliver suggests that a hunting accident might bring instantaneous death, but Spode replies that horse and rider are sometimes entangled.

The social atmosphere in the common-room is sharpened by the rough-hewn aggressiveness of Mr Bigwell, who prides himself on coming from the North and in being brought up as 'chapel'. It is softened by the pale and gentle Mr Dalziel, who announces that he is by religion a Catholic, which makes him unique among Compton-Burnett schoolmasters, and indeed among the whole range of her characters. From words on families and religion the masters move on to discuss their financial prospects, and then to wives and women in general. Mr Bigwell's statement that ' "a man is a man" ' is denied, on their own account, both by Spode and Oliver, who agree that neither, as a keeper of a boys' school, can Cassidy be a man, and that their meaning is 'simple not sinister'.

Simple yet sinister, Sefton finds the kind of scholastic triumphs expected of him by his parents to be incompatible with truth. He sacrifices the latter to the former, which leads him to make midnight sorties in search of the Latin cribs and arithmetic keys kept by Mr Bigwell and Mr Spode in their desks. It is Spode, making no bones of his need for a key to the sums worked by his pupils, who has uncovered Sefton's deceit. Bigwell is in a more difficult position as he has kept secret his reliance on classical cribs, so Bigwell is willing to support Sefton's fantasy that, possessing a supply of cribs, the boy has destroyed them from a feeling of guilt. This guilt, the headmaster decides, must feature in Sefton's school report, but Cassidy has another disciplinary problem to deal with before term ends.

Lucius, using an almost casual tone of voice, tells Spode and Oliver Shelley that the friendship between them is rather ' "too evident" '. At the time all parties concerned are standing in the passage. Juliet suggests that this is hardly the correct location for such a conversation, or, alternately, that the passage is the only place in which such matters could be spoken of. Oliver's comment is that he had thought, and even hoped, to meet this sort of thing on coming to the school, but had never expected to bring it with him. Spode mentions that they both bear the Christian name of Oliver, and, with her typical audacity, Juliet wonders how the friends address each other.

' "Perhaps they modify it in one case. But there are no names like Oliver, but Olivia. And that would not do. You need not look at me, Lucius. I said it would not do." '

Luckily, the understanding between Clemence and Sefton, when they meet in the holidays, brings them quickly to the point of finding that they are in the same predicament of waiting for their school reports to abase them before their parents. Their circumstances are made worse because their mother, in the blindly insensitive expectation of hearing an eulogy of her children, has invited Lesbia, Lucius and Juliet to spend Christmas among the Shelleys. Death or running away appear to be the only escape, but, as Clemence says, they would starve if they ran away and they have not the skill of savages to die when they wish. After her term's experience of Miss Firebrace, Clemence adds that only a civilised person could behave with the adroitness by which Lesbia makes things worse, apparently against her own will.

This is certainly Lesbia's attitude when she tells her tale to the parents, and the children are faced with their school reports. The tension of the scene slackens momentarily when old Mr Firebrace looks at these records of a term's deception, and is reminded of his own young days by the goings-on of the new generation. To his grandson Oliver's question, he replies that no one could have managed without cheating in his schooldays, everything being in Latin and Greek. And anyway the boys were only outwitting the masters and not each other. This glimpse of a coarser, if more realistic, age inspires Maria with the hope that her stepson Oliver may, in his schooldays, been as guilty as his half-brother and half-sister, but he regrets that the only comfort he can give Maria is to tell her of his

contemporary downfall by making ' "a conspicuous friendship" '. When Sir Roderick inquires if this friendship has
been with a boy, Oliver protests that both his father and his
grandfather are making an unnecessary display of a knowledge
of life, doubtless gained at first hand. But on realising that
the conspicuous friendship has been with another master,
Oliver Spode, Mr Firebrace shows a familiarity with the name
which is an indication of irregularities in conduct beyond
schoolboy cribbing.

In the meantime the children's predicament has to be
straightened out. With some reason, Sir Roderick says that as
the children never behaved dishonestly when at home, that is
the place to which they should return. Lesbia accuses him of
self-indulgence, but, finding Roderick resolved, takes the odd
trick by saying there are pains and penalties for this change
of plan.

' "Do you mean that we shall have to pay for next term, even
if they do not return?" '

This is precisely what Lesbia does mean, and her firmness
does not add to her popularity. Neither does her assumption
of amnesia when she is asked to state whether this levy will
include the extras. Financial affairs among the Shelleys do,
however, begin to look brighter when Maria, with a flourish,
hands her husband a wad of notes, product, she assures him, of
her savings. This gift is timely. A farm owned by Aldom's
mother, and formerly part of the estate, is believed to be
coming on the market, though Aldom plays a teasing game
with his master as to whether his mother is really willing to
sell. Aldom himself has had a setting-down from Clemence in
the schoolroom, where he has previously been a licensed
mimic. Sophisticated by her term at school, Clemence suddenly attacks Aldom for his mimicry of her mother, and for
the eavesdropping which provides him with his material.
Having attained a kind of moral puberty, Clemence goes on

to describe the school, not only as the scene of her humiliation, but as an initiation into a wider world, rich in specialist
education, and almost glamorous when everyone was dressed
in their best for the breaking-up party.

At this point in the book the plot of *Two Worlds and Their
Ways* ceases to run in a single stream, and splits, like a river
running across the sands towards the sea, into a number of
separate currents. New problems present fresh entanglements
when Oliver Firebrace announces that he expects a visit from
Oliver Spode. This prospect sets old Mr Firebrace off on a
chain of recollected memories about Spode's mother, a friend
of earlier days, known on terms of ' "give and take" '. Sir
Roderick suggests that the terms were ' "give" ', as his father-
in-law has made over money to a ' "Miss Spode" ', to help her
in the kind of trouble that is particularly hard for any Miss to
cope with. Mr Firebrace attempts some covering-up, with talk
of Mrs Spode and a defunct husband, though grateful to
Roderick for advancing him money for a purpose that has been
secret. Stimulated by talk of his friend of long age, Mr Firebrace now proposes to send by hand of Spode the pair of the
single ear-ring he had once given to Spode's mother. Oliver
intervenes to say that Spode was directed by his mother to
sell the single ear-ring, and that, by coincidence, someone had
come into the jeweller's shop with a duplicate. Although Mr
Firebrace declares that the ear-rings were unique, this turns
out impossible to prove because the ear-ring he has retained,
and its case, have disappeared from a drawer known, he
says, only to Oliver and himself. Sir Roderick points out that
this supposedly secret drawer is known, under that name, to
his wife and Aldom, as well as to himself. As Oliver says, it
seems kind of them to call it secret. Alarming speculation as
to how the jewel has vanished leads to mention of Aldom, a
suspicion protested against by Maria.
' "Neither Maria nor I wear earrings," said Lesbia.

"I suppose Aldom does not wear them either, . . ." [said Juliet].'

As the discussion of possible guilty persons gets ever less pleasant, Juliet leaves the room to fetch spectacles which are far from essential to her. She has only just returned to the centre of discussion when she points out a sparkle in a crack between the floorboards, a sparkle coming from the missing jewel. But the situation is still unresolved, because Mr Firebrace is certain that this ear-ring, having a distinguishing mark, is the one he has given to Spode's mother. Juliet's quickness of mind, habitually limited to making spiked remarks, now serves a practical purpose. She sends Maria, pale-faced and nervous, to rest, away from the company, before Spode's arrival. When this takes place, Spode's recognition of the ear-ring is instantaneous, but the scene is interrupted by Aldom announcing to Sir Roderick that Mrs Aldom, the butler's mother, is in the library to discuss the sale of her farm.

On meeting Mrs Aldom, Sir Roderick has the double shock of recognising her as his past mistress, and recognising that Aldom's intensely blue eyes are inherited from Roderick himself. Still staggering from this revelation, Roderick next perceives that there is a resemblance between his father-in-law, his eldest son and Oliver Spode, a resemblance that is beyond coincidence. The two love children for whose support the farm was sold are now, momentarily, under the same roof, and, when he has spoken to his father-in-law of Spode's genesis, Sir Roderick is left with the suspicion that Aldom's parentage has long been obvious to Mr Firebrace.

Drama piles itself on drama. Juliet tells Maria that she knows Maria has purloined the ear-ring to make a pair, Juliet having bought the ear-rings herself, under the impression that her father had sold them. Juliet has been helped in disentangling the history of the ear-rings, by recognising that Spode is her father's son, though a hint about this to Maria conveys nothing to the rather slow wits of the second Lady Shelley. In fact, unknown to Juliet, Maria is wrestling with a problem more painful to her than the sacrifice of her honesty in the interest of supplying her husband with a windfall. Resting concealed in the library she has overheard the talk between her husband and the mother of Aldom, and the shock has left her wondering if her sacrifice has been worthwhile.

A restless wish for action leads Maria to suggest that her children's former schoolmates should come for a day's visit, it being arranged that the boys should be brought by Miss James, the matron. Most parties concerned are agreed that Spode would be undesirable as a frequent visitor. During this exhausting day, Clemence finds that Esther has not abandoned her role as chief inquisitor, and the memories of Clemence's disgrace make for uneasiness. Sefton's friends are less probing, but it is through them that Maria's secret is revealed to more than Juliet. Keeping her promise that this secret will be safe with her, Juliet has not taken her husband into her confidence, so she does not foresee that Lucius will send Spode to escort Miss James and the little boys back to the school. Mr Firebrace welcomes his son with shameless pleasure, having earlier shown an interest, not entirely grandfatherly, in the more flirtatious of the schoolgirls. Spode, on his part, is now faced with Maria, and explains their joint sale of the ear-rings, one of which has been returned to Spode's mother. Maria keeps up a steady countenance until the school party leaves, which coincides with the sudden appearance of Juliet. When action is needed Juliet is bold in resource, and in order, as she says to ' "conduct the scene" ' she has halted an express train so that she can arrive at its inception. Juliet's explanation of Maria's stratagem certainly diminishes the general feeling that something reprehensible has taken place, though Lesbia is an exception, in revenge for Maria's attitude towards the standards of Lesbia's school. Oliver lists the positive advantages of Maria's action which, besides a farm for Roderick and another ear-ring for Spode's mother, include excitement for himself and his grandfather, a commodity undeniably scarce in their lives.

Alone with her husband, Maria tells him that she has overheard his talk with Mrs Aldom, and between themselves they settle that Aldom shall continue in their employment, unacknowledged, but one of a band of brothers. As Maria puts it, ' "I hope we are doing right, Roderick. If we are doing wrong, we must go on doing it. After all, we are used to it." '

Up in their schoolroom, the children are taking an equally desponding view of the future, until a bracing mimicry of one of the visiting school mistresses cheers their hearts.

' "Oh, we still have Aldom!" said Sefton. "He will always be here . . ."

"He heard the talk downstairs. He knows as much as we do now. He may soon know more. Things in his mind seem to grow." '

The book ends on this note, and, as ' "the talk downstairs" ' has included a comparison of the blue eyes of Sir Roderick with those of his butler, it seems likely that the things that grow in Aldom's mind may blossom into a full-blown domestic crisis.

Although there are no proposals of marriage in *Two Worlds and Their Ways*, sexual feelings are by no means discounted. Oliver admits that he took a post in a school with the idea that he might meet with romance, though he might, perhaps, have hesitated had he known that it would be with a half-uncle. Mr Firebrace and Sir Roderick, bereaved of their wives, lose little time in finding mistresses, the former going so far as to bestow his dead wife's jewellery on the mother of his illegitimate son. Both gentlemen are cheered by the sight of the schoolgirl visitors, dressed in their best and conscious of admiring males.

This is an excusable reaction, when the daily sight of Maria's weatherbeaten face and shabby clothes is underlined by Sir Roderick's habit of calling his wife ' "my pretty" '.

' "Those dear little boys!" said Maria. "I only just kept from embracing them."

"Grandpa kept from embracing several people," said Oliver. "I saw him keeping from it." '

In many Compton-Burnett novels the climax of the plot is reached before the last chapter, the drama being rounded off by a series of twists, sometimes startling to the reader, sometimes agonising to the author's less lovable characters. *Two Worlds and Their Ways* is an extreme example of this technique, for it is little more than half-way through the book when the children and their half-brother are back home, with their various ordeals left behind them as painful episodes in the lost world of school. The ill-deeds of their elders which come home to roost are not relevant to the children's own experience. The conjuring tricks by which one pair of ear-rings appears to multiply, the begetting of Spode and Aldom, their mother's well-intentioned theft, are of no concern to Clemence and Sefton. One of their worlds has proved too much for them, and it is only the Puck-like appearances of Aldom, half-brother by blood and entertainer by temperament, that illuminates the other stagnant world of home in which the children are now condemned to grow up.

14

THE FEMININE OF ŒDIPUS

Faced with the problem of finding surnames for her characters, Compton-Burnett had a strong predilection for patronymics with literary associations. It would, however, be over-subtle to suggest that, by bringing Bacon, Swift, Keats and Rosetti [sic] together in *More Women than Men*, the author adumbrated any of the qualities of their famous namesakes. Similarly Chaucer, Bunyan, Blake and Hallam (*Daughters and Sons*) exist without reflecting the talents of those from whom their names are borrowed. But the name of Hallam does seem to have struck Compton-Burnett as particularly suitable for a spinster earning her bread. Having been given to the most successful of Muriel Ponsonby's governesses (*Daughters and Sons*), it is used again in *Darkness and Day*, where a Miss Mildred Hallam is companion housekeeper to Sir Ransom Chace and his two unmarried daughters. This post is not considered full-time, nor is it paid as such, so that at the beginning of the book Mildred is seeking to supplement her salary by some part-time work outside the home.

Sir Ransom Chace, a rather dashing eighty-eight, is conscious that Miss Hallam is underpaid, but sees no reason to take steps to remedy the matter, beyond giving Mildred a bonus in the shape of benevolent politeness. He is less successful in restraining Jennet the parlourmaid, who, replacing the butler for reasons of economy, asks for and obtains a rise to two-thirds of that departed manservant's salary.

148

' "Of course the wages will ruin me," said Sir Ransom. "But so much does that, that I no longer notice it. Ruin must be like medicine and gradually cease to take effect." '

Jennet has addressed Sir Ransom when he and Mildred are alone in the early morning, cutting out any application to the daughters of the house, who now join an unusually relaxed Compton-Burnett breakfast-table. Not that relaxation plays much part in the life of Emma, the eldest daughter, whose tenseness includes an inclination to denigrate Mildred's household activities. Her instinct of resentment towards Miss Hallam turns out later to have an unexpectedly valid reason. Anne, the younger sister, is of a milder character, and, unlike Emma, appears to have accepted spinsterhood from choice and not from disappointed hopes. Family devotion has kept father and daughters calcified in their relation to each other, their behaviour to him being 'filial and hardly mature'.

The scene is interrupted by the arrival of Gaunt Lovat. He lives with his mother on an estate adjacent to Sir Ransom's and he has called to tell the Chaces that Edmund, his elder brother, Bridget, Edmund's wife, and their two little daughters are returning to live in the family home. Estrangement of an unexplained nature has caused their withdrawal, a particular deprivation to Sir Ransom whose affection for Bridget and her children is tenderer than the link that he is godfather to all of them can explain. Gaunt, a man in his fifties, cheers Sir Ransom by his visits, and the older man can even relish Gaunt's speculations as to what will happen to the estate after Sir Ransom's death, and that of his childless daughters. Gaunt's curiosity is a positive quality, but Sir Ransom takes pleasure in parrying the thrusts of inquiry, from whatever angle they come, denying any knowledge that his daughter Emma might have been willing to marry Gaunt's brother Edmund, and reproving Gaunt for assuming that death will come to Sir Ransom's daughters or even to himself.

Deprived of knowing the actual disposition of Sir Ransom's estate, Gaunt turns his imagination to the reading of the will, and forecasts the scene when the daughters will be grieving with decorum, and Miss Hallam uncertain ' "whether to be cheerful or not" '. Sir Ransom remarks that he appreciates the way Gaunt warms to his subject, but when Gaunt says that Edmund's children will be too young to attend the will-reading Sir Ransom asks how Gaunt knows they may not be grown-up when this occasion arises?

Miss Hallam's cheerfulness continues, unabated, throughout luncheon, and it is in this spirit that she offers, as a supplement to her wages, to teach Rose and Viola, the children who are returning to the home of the Gaunt family. Emma Chace, whose irritation at Mildred's irrepressible perkiness gives her an uncharitably clear eye, shows surprise that Mildred should feel her lack of experience to be no handicap in teaching these untamed children. It is now that the curious circumstances of Mildred's upbringing are revealed. An orphan, or so she understands, she has been brought up by a Miss Hallam, money having been provided to pay for her keep until she reached an age to support herself. After some probing by Gaunt, Sir Ransom admits that Bridget, Gaunt's sister-in-law, was also brought up by a Miss Hallam, a cousin of Mildred's foster mother. There has been a family quarrel, and the wards have never met. Mildred is firm that this cousinship by adoption will have no influence on her determined independence, nor on her undertaking to teach the little Lovats.

The home which is to be the scene of Mildred's additional labours is dominated by the widowed Selina Lovat, who sees no harm that Ambrose the butler should surprise herself and Gaunt locked in a somewhat over-affectionate embrace. Perhaps Gaunt needs some such outlet, having preferred to remain single in comfort rather than to marry on means inadequate for two. To the overwhelming curiosity which is the mainspring of his life, Gaunt adds a determination to allow no restraint to hinder him in analysing the information he collects, qualities which come into their own with the return of his brother's family. Unlike the Chaces, the Lovats, as has been noted, can still afford a butler. They also employ a cook, Mrs Spruce, whose devotion to Bridget Lovat causes remark, and with good reason. Ambrose has an assistant, Bartle, less agonised than his counterpart in *Manservant and Maidservant*, but equally rebellious at his destiny, and armed with more weapons of malice. Tabby, the between-maid, is barely visible to the naked eye, but has good nature disproportionate to her size, while Alice, the tall housemaid, is chiefly concerned with her own dignity. It should not be overlooked that, however large a Compton-Burnett household may be, the employers invariably regard themselves as in straitened circumstances, as indeed they usually are. Relatively affluent heads of families, such as Horace Lamb (*Manservant and Maidservant*) or Felix Bacon's father (*More Women than Men*) manage to achieve a false impression of poverty by stinting the dependants who are at their mercy.

The homecoming of Edmund and Bridget is darkened by Edmund's announcement that the morning will bring forth a revelation, soul-shattering, but necessary before the communal family life can be resumed. Rose and Viola do not help the reunion by a covert discussion on what flowers would be a suitable adornment for their grandmother's grave. On the other hand, the welcome of Sir Ransom for Bridget and her children brings a glow to the occasion, duplicated by the equally affectionate greeting of Mrs Spruce, the cook. Fanshawe, nurse to the children, is welcomed back into the life of the kitchen, where she paints a gloomy picture of the family she serves, a mother in a melancholy dream, a father unable to do anything but jest, two children spoilt but forlorn.

This situation is illustrated before the evening's end, by the need to summon the entire drawing-room party to staunch Viola's tears at the strangeness of a home she has half-forgotten.

The following morning brings the history of Edmund and Bridget's trouble, a woe vast as it is incurable. As a young man Edmund has had an affair with a girl on a local farm. (Willing young girls seem to be the most fertile products of Compton-Burnett farms. Even Mrs Aldom (*Two Worlds and Their Ways*) found the farm she had acquired by losing her virtue too hard a struggle to work profitably.) Edmund assures his mother and his brother Gaunt that this encounter was a casual one, though it resulted in pregnancy. Although settling some money on the coming child, to support it through its dependent years, Edmund has, unadmirably, been more concerned with secrecy than parental responsibility. Years later he married Bridget, an orphan, brought up in a neighbouring village, a goddaughter and protégée of Sir Ransom Chace.

Only after the birth of Rose and Viola has Edmund come across the parents of the girl he got with child, to learn that she died at the baby's birth. He has learnt, too, that the child was a daughter, and that she was adopted by a Miss Hallam. Husband and wife, concluding that they are father and daughter, have now been condemned to live as brother and sister. Margaret Mead, the anthropologist, wrote of the incest taboo, that sex relations are forbidden between certain persons, born because sex is permitted, even required, of other persons. Trapped by both aspects of this taboo, Edmund regards the situation as no worse than unfortunate, but Bridget, brooding and haunted, has only returned to her husband's family on condition that the story is made plain.

Selina Lovat faces this involuntary complication of blood relationships among her descendants, by asking why Edmund had never confided in his mother, and then by addressing

Bridget as her daughter, for what else can she call her? Her daughter-in-law and granddaughter's reply is to comment on the nobility of people under test, adding that she and Edmund have been sufficiently brave not to put out their own eyes.
' "Perhaps people are braver than they used to be." '

Sending Edmund and Bridget from the library to allow them the outlet of private discussion, Selina and Gaunt have their own relief in speaking plainly of this new limitation, or doubling up, of their family circle. Gaunt proceeds to examine the parallel in classical legend, pointing out that Bridget has done and suffered the fate of Œdipus as nearly as a woman could, causing her mother's death at her birth and marrying her father. Selina agrees that Bridget has shown restraint in not putting out her eyes, and in not imitating Œdipus by going about from town to town spreading the terrible news, though no one, Selina says, seems to have thought it odd of Œdipus at the time.

Throughout the discussion of her peculiar origins, Rose has been hiding behind the library sofa. Still unseen, she slips upstairs where Fanshawe and Viola are awaiting Mildred Hallam's debut as a daily governess. In the pause before Mildred's arrival, Rose explains that she has been imprisoned in the library by a lengthy grown-up conversation, and, having a rudimentary acquaintance with classical legend, she is able to interpret what she has heard so as to make it only too comprehensible to Fanshawe. Viola is slightly baffled by the physiological aspects of her mother's birth, which Rose mentions as an occasion on which mothers sometimes die from no fault of their babies.
' "A baby couldn't kill anyone," said Viola, kicking up her feet. "It would be too small." '

These preliminaries do not lead to a happy beginning with Mildred. In a passage of governess-baiting which lasts for seven pages, the children persist in painting, and refuse to accept any instruction, with a success that other tormentors of their instructresses in Compton-Burnett schoolrooms would regard with respect.

Fanshawe descends to the kitchen ostensibly to arrange that the children should have tea with Mrs Spruce, but with the deeper need to halve the burden of Rose's communication by sharing it with the senior domestics. With distressful haste, Mrs Spruce at once tells her colleagues that she knows there has been a misapprehension. She takes it much amiss when she finds in them a reluctance to believe her word. Alice, the housemaid, and Fanshawe, show what Mrs Spruce considers a reprehensible satisfaction in ' "the sufferings of the innocent" '. In the grip of painful emotions, Mrs Spruce writes a letter, which she posts by her own hand, rebuffing an offer to do so from the blatantly curious Bartle.

Unfortunately, while Rose and Viola are being entertained at tea in the kitchen, the talk turns on relationships. Rose speaks aloud the thoughts she has worked out, explaining that she and her sister can have fewer relations than most people, only one grandfather instead of two, because their father himself would be one of them. Like a hawk when his prey breaks cover, Bartle pounces on this explanation of the cloud over the house and the banishment of Tabby and himself to take their tea apart. Ambrose sternly tells his underling to hold his tongue, Alice adding that question of where Bartle has his tea is a minor point. This is the first, but not the last, occasion when Bartle is to find that the revelation of wrong-doing among his supposed superiors leads to no slackening of the firmness with which he is snubbed. Over-excited by an orgy of toastmaking at the kitchen fire, Viola whispers to her mother that Mrs Spruce has denied the story of Bridget's parentage. The Lovats thus become aware that their most shameful secret is now known to every member of their household.

Fortunately, as a reviewer of *Darkness and Day* wrote in *The Times Literary Supplement* on the book's appearance, things are not quite so bad as they appear. The following morning, after the day of anguish, Sir Ransom Chace receives a letter which gives him a shock he cannot conceal, distressing him to a degree which enables Emma to take the letter from him. Emma says that the childish handwriting of the letter suggests a tenant, but the contents are far from childish, exploding like a bomb in the face of Sir Ransom, and even more harshly in the face of his daughter. The letter, in making it plain that Edmund is not Bridget's father presents the inescapable inference that he is the father of Mildred. Faced with evidence of Edmund's preference for anyone except herself, Emma only regains her balance when Mildred insists that the sudden acquisition of a father, a grandmother, an uncle and two half-sisters will make no change in her own situation as governess in the house of a galaxy of kinsfolk. In this spirit, Mildred sets out on her daily task, bearing a letter from Sir Ransom with incontrovertible evidence that she, and not Bridget, is Edmund's daughter. Apart from saying that he knew Bridget's parents, Sir Ransom points out that Bridget has money settled on her by her father, while Mildred has had no such permanent provision made for her. Anne Chace wishes it were possible to say that Edmund is fortunate to have Mildred, but Emma is determined that Mildred must be considered to have no cause for complaint. Edmund, she says, has discharged his obligations many years before.

' "Would you have seen them like that, Father?" (said Anne). "No, my dear. But I am a law to no one else." '

How truly Sir Ransom speaks becomes apparent soon afterwards. In the meantime, when Edmund has read the letter brought by Mildred, he is not prepared to take such a detached view of this new-found daughter as Emma has hoped. After a particularly stormy session with the children, which includes the setting of a chair for Mildred that collapses under her, the warmth of Edmund's recognition is soothing, though Mildred firmly retains the formal address which, she says, is to be her custom when she meets her father. Edmund agrees, but on this one day, to make amends for past neglect, gathers Mildred into an embrace, which is witnessed by Tabby the midget between-maid.

The natural misunderstanding that arises when Tabby, without undue drama, reports this incident to the assembled staff, gives Bartle an opportunity for some barbed remarks about the dubious goings-on above stairs. On the other hand, Alice, learning from Tabby that both parties to the embrace "seemed solemn" ', interprets the scene as one of renunciation, and so to be respected. The matter is cleared up by the arrival of Jennet, the Chace's parlourmaid, who has taken the precautions of overhearing the circumstances of Bridget's birth, as described by Sir Ransom. Having passed this news on, Jennet elucidates the other half of the mystery surrounding the adopted daughters of two Miss Hallams.

' ". . . Mr Edmund was a father before he should have been."
(said Jennet)
"It is generally a woman who is that," said Bartle.'

Jennet has taken advantage of her afternoon out to tell her tale to the Lovat domestics, and so the responsibility of organising the tea-party, at which the Lovats are being entertained by the Chaces, falls on Mildred. Emma has learnt that Mildred has had a meeting with her father, and works off some of her spleen by making it clear that Mildred is not to be present as an equal at the tea-party. But she underestimates Mildred's ubiquity, a continual bobbing-up on errands of hospitality, culminating in the removal of some Dresden tea-cups, whose washing she reserves for herself. Demonstrating the china's delicacy, Mildred remains undaunted at breaking a cup; this accident and Mildred's demeanour causes

Emma to remark that self-control when at fault oneself is a suitable quality for one engaged in the management of children. Gaunt continues to bite on the aching tooth of Mildred's situation and the propriety of her leaving the neighbourhood, but Edmund's counter-attack, that it is really Gaunt, with his uncontrollable tongue, who should go away, is halted by the signs that a final fading has come upon Sir Ransom. Lying on what is to be his deathbed, he asks to see Bridget and her children, together with Emma and Anne, so that he may take a last look at the five who, he says, he leaves behind.

Sir Ransom is glad that Gaunt keeps his interest in the disposition of the estate until the patriarch's last moments. With Sir Ransom dead, Gaunt's awareness that his inquisitiveness will soon be satisfied puts him in such a state of pitiable excitement that, as Bridget says, it appears he will not hear the will read after the funeral, being likely to die of curiosity before the day. Such a fate is averted by Gaunt himself, who manoeuvres so that he is allowed to read the will immediately. To the surprise of the company, Sir Ransom has left his property between his daughters and Bridget, settling the estate on Bridget's children.

Returning the will to the desk in which it has been kept, Gaunt reaches the climax of a career devoted to satisfying curiosity by opening a packet, unfamiliar to the family. This packet contains not only a photograph of Bridget as a small child on the knee of an unknown woman, but a letter, in the same handwriting as the letter which rescued Edmund and Bridget from their illusion of incest. This older letter states explicitly that Bridget is Sir Ransom's daughter. At her first glance at the photograph, Selina at once suspects who must be Bridget's mother, and, with quickness and kindliness somewhat alien to her character, manages to cast the photograph into the fire, with the acquiescence of the family.

Mildred now joins the scene as an actor, having previously been an unsuspected onlooker. It is she who has tidied the desk and brought the photograph to the surface, an additional aggravation to Emma, who can tolerate Mildred's knowledge of her father's secret even less than the inescapable fact that Mildred, although illegitimate, is now a connection of the Chace family.

Emma's exasperation at Mildred is shared by Miss Hallam's own pupils (and half-sisters). Their bland disregard of their governess as anything but a nuisance, reduces her to a state when she can agree with Edmund that she would be happier elsewhere. Without using those words, the father and daughter indicate to each other that Emma's jealousy would also cause general unhappiness. The result of this consultation is exactly the opposite to Emma's own desire. Edmund proposes to give Mildred an allowance, which will liberate them both to meet in their true relationship. Selina is also willing to welcome another granddaughter, all the more so because Edmund and Bridget will have no more children. Having practised the continence prescribed by their supposed relationship, the pair find that they have become to each other what they had imagined themselves to be. Although Œdipus Rex might be said to have given way to A Comedy of Errors, there remains the side-effect that Edmund's wife has become his daughter, in feeling if not in blood. His daughters by blood have one last scene of farewell, at the end of which Rose remarks, in a world-weary manner, that another chapter has been closed, but she would prefer a governess who did not expect ' "so much feeling" '.

With their skill in eavesdropping, there is every reason to suppose that the children will learn that Mildred is their father's daughter, and it is a sad loss that their comments on this discovery can only be imagined. But eavesdropping plays its part in one final revelation. Jennet arrives in Mrs Spruce's kitchen with the news that Sir Ransom has fathered an illegitimate daughter, now the daughter-in-law of their employer. Heads are shaken, with gloomy relish, but Mrs Spruce takes the charitable point of view that there is a cause for gladness in the revelation of Sir Ransom's lapse being post mortem. Bartle challenges Mrs Spruce by asking what ' "the old sinner" ' had to do with her, seeming to receive a vibration from Mrs Spruce unfelt by others in the kitchen. After seeing Jennet out, Mrs Spruce meets Selina in the hall, and as they look at each other the knowledge that they share one last family secret passes unspoken between them. Bracing herself for whatever may come, Mrs Spruce goes to her bedroom and takes from her chest a copy of the photograph of Bridget as a child, on the knee of an unknown girl, the photograph of which Selina has already burnt Sir Ransom's copy. Mrs Spruce can still trace her own young face as she looks in the glass and compares the photograph with the 'full, florid face' she now possesses. Selina is, however, entirely equal to this new development. Still waiting for Mrs Spruce in the hall, she adds to the information that Sir Ransom's daughters will be spending the following day with the Lovats, the request, more an assertion than a question, that Mrs Spruce will do her best for the family as she always has in the past and always will in the future. Mrs Spruce assents without undue emotion, but both the grandmothers of Rose and Viola are aware that a compact has been made between them, which brings the book to an end on a note of unexpected stability.

Darkness and Day shares, to some extent, with *Two Worlds and Their Ways* that split in plot caused by the early resolution of a crisis, though in *Darkness and Day* there is less slackening of tension. In the unfolding of Bridget's history, clues can be picked up from Mrs Spruce's fondness for Bridget her affectionate interest in Rose and Viola, and from Bartle's instinct that a mystery attaches to Mrs Spruce. Bartle is not as cosmically curious as Gaunt, but he rebels, not unreasonably, at the fate which has led him to be subservient to those who have done what he has been taught to regard as reprehensible. Bartle is more aggressively unpleasant than George in *Manservant and Maidservant*, but, undeniably, he possesses higher moral standards.

At a first reading the plot of *Darkness and Day* may seem to depend too heavily on the coincidence of the two Miss Hallams each adopting a child, quarrelling and ceasing to meet. The cause of the quarrel is unexplained but at the period of which Compton-Burnett principally wrote family feuds carried an edge, razor-sharp to cut blood ties. It would be absurd to suggest that such severances lie only in the past, but the last quarter of the nineteenth century seems to have been particularly fertile soil for the growth of family feuds in cramped social circles, perhaps from a need to dramatise lives often dull to the point of suffocation. If the question of the two Miss Hallams and their adopted children can be accepted, there is still the plethora of eavesdropping, and the ill-advised retention of photographs as obstacles to the suspension of scepticism. Eavesdropping and overhearing are devices which Compton-Burnett never hesitated to use for her purposes. And again the opportunities for these rewarding activities were considerably greater in the days when houses and households were larger. The part that photographs can play in undesired revelation has already been seen in *Daughters and Sons* and in *Parents and Children*. Also to be met with in later novels, the hoarding of these instruments of betrayal might be thought to show a subconscious desire to be found out. However, those who have sorted the possessions of a deceased person would agree that the instinct not to destroy photographs is ingrained in some natures. Having offered reasons for the acceptance of coincidence in various forms, it must be admitted that in *Darkness and Day* there is a lapse seldom to be met with in Compton-Burnett novels. On one occasion it is difficult to be certain to whom some lines of dialogue should be attributed, in a conversation among the Chace family. In this passage someone, most likely Anna Chace, a faint but benevolent character, remarks, ' "I like people to be fortunate. It makes the world more cheerful." '

Good fortune and cheerfulness are mostly remarkable by their absence in *The Present and The Past*, the novel which followed *Darkness and Day*.

15

WOLF! WOLF!

The sun of good fortune has not shone on Cassius Clare, the male lead rather than the hero of *The Present and The Past*. His limited social circle has not prevented him from finding wide opportunities to make himself unhappy. Cassius may qualify for a niche in the Compton-Burnett pantheon of domestic tyrants, but it would be in a lowly position, suitable for one who lacks the single-minded egotistical drive to maintain an unquestioned rule. Cassius exacts love and fear in inadequate quantities. In the end the two people who love him most—his father and Ainger his butler—allow him to die, wrongly assuming that he is, for the second time, faking a suicide to attract the pity of his family.

The book opens with the younger Clare children watching a flock of hens, attacking one of their number who has fallen sick. Henry Clare has a habit of greeting unpleasantness with the words ' "Oh dear, oh dear," ' in this case using them to show sympathy for the sick hen's sufferings under the pecking of the flock. Henry and his sister Megan, aged eight and seven, have a reaction to this tragedy of the hen-yard that is a contrast to the behaviour of their three-year old brother Toby, who shares his morning snack of cake with the hens and only becomes slightly discomposed when the sick bird has what Henry calls ' "death-pangs" '. Except for a willingness to share his cake, Toby's behaviour as the spoilt baby of the Clare family makes that of Neville Sullivan (*Parents and Children*) appear positively unselfish

On this particular morning the nerves of the household are on edge, because Catherine, the first wife of Cassius and the mother of his two eldest sons, is due to return to the neighbourhood after an absence of nine years. Miss Ridley, the governess responsible for the elder children, endeavours to maintain an ordinary manner, but Fabian, now thirteen and so four when his mother left, is disturbed because he can remember her, and Guy, only two at the time, is disturbed because he cannot. To Guy's question as to what a real mother is like, Fabian replies that she is like their stepmother with her own children. When Miss Ridley protests that no difference is made, Fabian goes on to say that the difference is there, and does not need to be made. He adds, replying to a further question of Guy's, that no father is like their father, and so they have no normal parent. With an effort of loyalty, Miss Ridley says that Cassius is devoted to his sons in his way, and Fabian replies.

' "I dare say a cat does the right thing to a mouse in its way." '

Luncheon in the dining-room brings a clash between Cassius and Flavia, his second wife, in which Cassius's father Mr Clare acts as umpire. Mr Clare has presumably bestowed the name of Cassius on his son, but his own *prénom* is not apparent. Flavia and Mr Clare have refused to respond to Cassius's suggestion that luncheon is a meal that could be dispensed with. After complaining that Flavia has an unusually large appetite, Cassius toys with a shred of meat to support his theory of the superfluity of eating at midday and then gives himself a normal helping, catching his wife's eye as he does so. ' "Having my luncheon after all," he said as if quoting his wife's thought.'

This sensitivity to the thoughts of others does not lead

Cassius to modify his behaviour in his struggle with life. He has, absentmindedly, given himself a second helping of the meal he has condemned, when he is brought a letter from his first wife, Catherine. The impact of the Past on the Present excites Cassius almost to flirtatiousness. He refuses the suggestion that he should read Catherine's letter aloud, on the grounds that his father and his present wife will make sniping remarks. He does not wish to be treated as a culprit, when he is a man married to two wives at once. Requested to be explicit, Cassius asks if it would be more explicit to be married to ten wives. To which Flavia replies that it would be less explicit, and require more explanation.

Catherine's letter holds a request that she may have access to her sons, with the threat that she will take her own means of seeing them if this is denied to her. Her former husband, in his cultivation of new grievances, comes near to complaining that she makes no mention of wishing to see him. He even brings the matter up in a confidential chat with Ainger, the butler. Like Mortimer Lamb (*Manservant and Maidservant*) Cassius finds such talks to be a solace, but in Cassius's case the balm of Ainger's conversation soothes the irritation caused by his wife and children. Darts are perpetually planted in the hump of Cassius's self-esteem, even by Toby, whose overdeveloped habit of blaming others for his own misdeeds causes his father to prohibit the child being told anything but facts. Cassius finds little support for his attitude from his wife, and their daughter Megan chillingly comments that it seems to be a pity that, when two women were prepared to marry her father, he liked being married to neither of them.

The powers of Toby's imagination are even more clearly displayed to Cassius when he comes upon his children, Eliza the nurserymaid and William the gardener, all on their knees before the grave that has been dug for a mole. Toby has already announced that he will have a church when he grows

up, but that only men like his father, and not gardeners like
William, will be allowed to attend it. He has, however, waived
'the question of the class of his congregation in favour of
its size'. Toby's fluency in his own version of the burial
service, ' "Ashes and ashes. Dust and dust . . . Poor little mole!
Until he rise again. . . ." ' causes pain to Cassius, but only
admiration to Bennet the children's nurse. With a feeling
that his world is uniting against him, Cassius next examines
the elegant poem that Megan has written for the mole's
obsequies. The first line 'My name is Mole,' recalls something
to Cassius. Although he does not remember Blake's poem
'Joy is my name' with any accuracy, this does not prevent
him from accusing Megan of plagiarism. As the family leave
the mole's grave, Megan says that there is not, in her opinion,
much to be understood about her father. ' "When he is unhappy himself he wants other people to be." '

The servants' hall in Cassius's house is well-populated, but
only Ainger, the butler, plays an active part in the development of the story through his traffic with his employers. Mrs
Frost, the cook, has a sardonic opinion of her situation in
life, but Halliday, the general man, takes an even dourer view
of his more lowly position, having advanced no further in
fifty years of a servitude begun as page-boy. The present
page-boy, Simon, is very unlike George (*Manservant and
Maidservant*) or Bartle (*Darkness and Day*). His first
appearance in the suit of buttons worn by Ainger twenty
years before, is a stimulation to Kate and Madge, the two
housemaids. They find no emotional release in each other,
and any hope of catching Ainger as a husband is discounted
by the concentration of the butler's interest on his master.
Undeterred by the depressing spectacle of Halliday's failure
to mount the domestic ladder, Simon is ambitious to rise by
hard work and thrift. He gets an early lesson in the cruelty
of life in the shape of a practical joke played by horrible

little Toby. Finding that blaming others, in words, for his own wrong-doing leads to contradiction and reproof, the youngest son of the house deliberately breaks a vase, unobserved by his elders and then conveys the impression that Simon is the culprit, an action all the more sinister from being carried out in dumbshow.

The servants in Cassius's household have their part as chorus, but there are two other commentators close at hand. In a house described by Cassius as having books all over it and little else, the return of Catherine is awaited by her brother and sister, Ursula and Elton Scrope. Their state of contentment and Elton's literary tendencies recall some of the happier pairs in *Brothers and Sisters*, though Elton's fear of publishing his work in case it should be read has more in common with Lester Marlow's attitude to his writing. (*Parents and Children*) Catherine sweeps down upon this peaceful nest with the authority of one who has brought up her younger brother and sister, and with no questioning of her right to leave and enter the lives of others as her own feelings dictate. The threads of the old relationship are being gathered together when Cassius comes to call, unable to resist a sight of his first wife. Apparently he bears no grudge that Catherine had once found life with him so intolerable that she was prepared to sacrifice her children to escape from it. There is, incidentally, no mention of any co-respondent who may have been cited in the divorce between Cassius and Catherine. If there had been such a man, it would be in keeping with Catherine's character to have treated him as totally disposable.

Naturally the immediate discussion is about an arrangement for Catherine to see her sons, and about Flavia's attitude to the matter. Cassius, in his manic mood, insists that he will not be bound by the past, and that he has imposed this view on Flavia, in a way which, he says, Catherine will doubtless remember. Catherine remembers only too well, and

166

before she leaves her brother and sister alone, after Cassius's departure, she tells them that she makes no claim to Cassius's kind of generosity. Ursula and Elton speculate nervously how they are to manage two lives, when one is barely in their compass. But Elton is also haunted by the obvious appeal that Catherine still has for her former husband, and wonders if a faithful heart beats under an unpromising exterior.

Cassius takes his problematically faithful heart back to his own house, where he feels he is getting too little sympathy from his second wife when, in expectation of applause, he describes his visit to his first.

' "... So I took the bull by the horns and walked up to the cannon's mouth." ' After this splendidly surrealist mixture of metaphors, Cassius goes on to say that this action has brought out deep qualities in himself. He becomes incensed at Flavia's obvious distaste for his pæan of self-praise, and complains that no other man would have come back from the greatest effort of his life to be greeted by such a lack of appreciative enthusiasm. Cassius is not the greatest of Compton-Burnett buffoons, but he has enough of the quality to explain the attachment and concern that he arouses in his father and his butler.

The meal at which Catherine meets her sons passes off with no more embarrassment than Toby taking an undue fancy to the strange lady whom his elder brothers call 'Mother'. There is regret among the domestic staff that such decorum has prevailed, and in a pining for excitement Madge, one of the housemaids, says she wishes they had done something common or mean ' "upon that memorable scene" '. This quotation leads Simon forward in his literary and historical education, when he inquires who had so behaved. It was someone, he is told, who was to be beheaded, when it would be hard to be oneself.

' "Anyhow for long," said Mrs Frost.'

While her staff are displaying an edifying familiarity with Andrew Marvell's *Horatian Ode*, Flavia is behaving ever less commonly and meanly. Overcoming a reluctance to allow Catherine to see her sons at will, Flavia goes to tell her predecessor that she may do exactly that. Catherine has gauged correctly that Flavia's standard is too high for her to jib at sacrificing her own position with the boys she has brought up. Catherine offers thanks for what she describes as an escape from bitterness, and also from the sadness of self-pity. Reflections on this theme, that people are enjoined to pity others but blamed for pitying themselves, mark the beginning of a friendship between Flavia and Catherine, soon to be a cause of complaint from the man they have both married. Indeed self-pity, ever powerful with Cassius, now takes possession of him, for he finds that he has lost both his wives to each other.

As usual muddled in his thinking, Cassius rails to his father about the absurd twist of fate which makes his first and second wives neutralise each other, leaving their husband a neglected bystander. Mr Clare can only reply that Cassius has earlier said that he might be keeping a harem, and that he cannot see how his son would have managed one. Mr Clare has reason on his side, for Cassius goes on to complain that the two women being absorbed in each other is unwholesome, ' "apart from them being wives of the same man. It may set tongues to work." '

With these sinister reflections on the friendship between Flavia and Catherine, *The Present and The Past* moves into a tragic phase, with Cassius's manic depression becoming wholly depressive. With the knowledge that his father relies on pills of which ten would be a fatal dose, Cassius begins to be fascinated by the idea of his own suicide, and the shock of remorse it would bring to the survivors. He hardly attends to Mr Clare's comment that Cassius himself would not be there to appreciate his family's grief. The sense of isolation increases to the unbearable, when Cassius comes upon a harmonious group of his two wives and five children, a group from which he is separated by his own personality, whose members increase his resentment by giving him what he sees as scraps of attention.

It has been suggested earlier that it is the element of the buffoon in Cassius which has won the devotion of Ainger, and it is Ainger who feels immediate self-reproach when Cassius is discovered unconscious, having taken a heavy dose of his father's pills. The doctor's care snatches Cassius back to life, and gives Ainger an opportunity to moralise on his own feelings which are very different from those of Halliday the general man. This Thersites of the servants' hall, when he hears that Cassius is well enough for an interview with his wife and his father, says that Cassius would have something to listen to if he, Halliday, was in their place.

In fact Halliday has made an accurate guess at the tone of the interview, for neither Mr Clare nor Flavia are prepared to accept that a vague despair was Cassius's only motive for taking a nearly fatal dose of his father's pills. The situation is still unresolved when the children arrive, and Cassius's discomposure is increased by Henry's inquiry when his father complains that had he done a ' "good action" ' it would have remained unknown. ' "Have you ever done one?" said Henry. "You know I don't mean you haven't. I just wanted to know." ' In the meantime Toby, always acquisitive, has found a bottle that he requires to be rattled for his amusement. Mr Clare claims the bottle as his own, and says it is nearly empty, no good for rattling, which Toby demonstrates to be untrue. The pills remaining in the bottle do not tally with the number Cassius is supposed to have swallowed, and it becomes evident that he has been enjoying under false pretences, the sympathy due to despair.

Cassius's own reaction is that the whole episode is the fault of those who have left him to loneliness, and he is not entirely disappointed with the scene he has made. When Flavia says the affair must not be spoken of outside the house, Cassius agrees that things must be kept in proportion, but with some complacency at the idea of being the subject of gossip—if not a hero—though he acknowledges that this is not a state that lasts indefinitely. He finds it difficult to accept that to his family he has planned a deception, a proceeding his children know he would have condemned in them. However, Cassius, putting out a fifth leg as a horse is said to do in an emergency, waves aside awkwardness by saying the children are shown to have had a sound training in morals from their parents. At this moment it becomes obvious that Ainger has been doing a little dilettante dusting in the background. The butler returns to his fellows below stairs, with a relish for the news which he has his master's permission to pass on. Simon remarks that, coming to help Ainger, he has seen the butler standing in concentrated idleness outside the library door, but is assured that, far from being idle, Ainger was doing his duty, odd as it may seem to Simon.

Another oddness Simon has had to learn is that an atmosphere of politeness in the dining-room at breakfast is to Ainger a storm signal, boding ill for the tenor of the day. Ainger says that he often waits by the breakfast table with his heart standing still and his blood running cold. This state of frigid suspension does not, however, prevent Ainger from joining in the conversation of his employers', on a morning when Cassius is off his feed and indulging in a mood of persecuted withdrawal. Asked if he would wish to attend the village flower-show, Ainger replies that he is familiar with the exhibits entered from the Clare's garden, so he has no wish to see the other entries should they be inferior, and still less should they chance to be superior. Ainger's philosophy of self-contemplation gives no lift to Cassius's depressed spirits. Alone at his desk he seems unable to grapple with the routine of normal business, bringing a long-neglected order for wine and an envelope in proximity, without being able to make the connecting gesture.

Flavia has left the house to visit Catherine, so it is to Mr Clare that, two hours later, Ainger reports that Cassius is once more unconscious on the library sofa. The two people who have, so far, supported Cassius's moods with generous tolerance agree that this is yet another cry of Wolf! Wolf!, and that wisdom suggests Cassius should be left to revive, in his own time, from a second under-dose. By the time Flavia returns Ainger has realised that his diagnosis has been rash. The doctor arrives, but it is now too late for stimulants, which might have rallied Cassius from the illness of the heart that has struck him. The sick hen, pecked by its family, with which the story began, has been the symbol of Cassius's view of his own situation. Now he dies, and the general behaviour reminds the reader of the mole's obsequies.

Flavia's self-reproach is divided between regrets that her stiff and absolute standard prevented her from giving Cassius the flattery that was all he needed, and fears that her friendship with Catherine has been a pernicious influence in her family life. But Cassius's death is only the first step in the disintegration of the home. Catherine declares that her return has been responsible for too much damage, and therefore she will leave the neighbourhood. Flavia puts the choice to Catherine's sons, and Fabian chooses his real mother, while Guy, his heart torn in two, cannot bear not to go with his brother. Megan raises a wail, which finds echoes in other hearts, that each time Fabian and Guy return everybody will have changed, until the change becomes too great for knowledge of each other.

The only people to suffer no pangs in the painful upheaval are Ursula and Elton. It is left to them to sum up the story after Catherine has told them that she will be removing her unlucky presence. She may be trailing remorse behind her, but she has her sons as trophies. Her brother and sister are aware that she has achieved a good deal for someone who has professed to ask for nothing. Catherine herself is unaware of the profound relief her departure has caused to Ursula and Elton. Ursula asks her brother whom he pities most ' "in the whole sad tale" '.

' "Cassius, because he is dead. Guy has lost a mother; Flavia a friend; the children have lost a father. But he has lost himself." '

It might be added that Mr Clare has lost a son, and Ainger a friend as well as a master.

The two novels preceding *The Present and The Past* belong to a monochrome phase of Compton-Burnett's work, and to a certain extent this book shares some of the qualities of grisaille rather than the lustre of oil paint. Cassius is an exception among the characters. Painted in full colour, his death is not only the climax of the novel and the cause of the dissolution of his family as a unit; it is the end of the book of which he is almost the hero he would like to have been.

16

POSITIVE COMPANIONSHIP

Mother and Son opens with the mother of the title, Miranda
Hume, interviewing a prospective companion, Miss Burke,
who has answered an advertisement for the situation. Miranda
is a despotic octogenarian, with a stranglehold over her son
Rosebery, this grip on her middle-aged offspring being, presumably, her compensation for the pains of bearing and
rearing. Miranda has taken the precaution to secure
Rosebery's devoted service, but the rest of her household
shows more of a leaning towards negative rebellion than
positive companionship. Julius, Miranda's husband, has been
elbowed out of the centre of her life by her concentration on
Rosebery. In consequence, Julius has developed a sardonic
detachment towards his wife, his feelings being held by his
orphaned nephews and niece. These three children range
from Francis, a mature fifteen, to Adrian, an immature twelve,
with Alice in between as the jam in the sandwich. Julius has
given the orphans both a home and his love. Miranda has
acquiesced in giving them the former, but has offered them
only a tolerance verging on the grudging. Lacking the
savagery of Sabine Ponsonby (*Daughters and Sons*) and the
sexual passions of Josephine Napier (*More Women than Men*),
Miranda still manages to put on a good show of bullying the
young on one hand, and parental possessiveness on the other.
Not surprisingly, Mrs Hume's ideas of companionship are

difficult of fulfilment. Her interview with Miss Burke starts by a stubborn auctioning up of the applicant's age, from ' "over thirty" ' by way of ' "not much under forty" ' to the true figure of forty-seven. After an exchange on the tone of voice to be used for reading aloud, Miranda decides the matter can be carried no further. As the scene has been watched from close at hand by Rosebery, and from across the room by the rest of the family, there is a feeling that matters have already gone too far. Miss Burke salvages what dignity she can by inquiring if Mrs Hume has ever had a companion before, and fires a parting shot by pointing out the impossibility of Miranda's requirements being satisfied.

Sharing Miss Burke's doubts, Alice murmurs that her aunt should advertise for a martyr, and Miranda reproves the children for sniggering in corners ' "like stable boys" '.

' ". . . I did not know that stable boys sniggered," said Alice. "They always seem so grave."

"They certainly swear very earnestly," said [Francis].'

While the question of stableboys' habits is under discussion, the failed applicant for the situation as martyr has been given tea by Bates, the parlourmaid, who recommends another situation in a neighbouring household of two spinster friends. Proceeding on this new quest, Miss Burke is chaperoned on her way by Rosebery, whose intense devotion to his mother is large enough to include all other women. His courteous act has been observed by Mr Pettigrew, the discomforts of whose post as daily tutor are increased by his pupils' bad manners at tea-time, and their ribaldry whenever he refers to himself as a gentleman. This over-developed class-consciousness may be the result of Miranda's insistence that a bleak future of toiling for bread faces the children, but it makes them appear pathetic rather than attractive. On this particular evening they have the additional enjoyment, besides mocking Mr Pettigrew's insistent claims to gentlemanliness, of making fun of his determination to refer to Miss Burke, the repudiated prospective companion, as everything except a lady.

Miss Burke, herself, has fallen on her feet, by scaling down her pretensions from companion to working housekeeper. Her employers, Emma Greatheart and Hester Wolsey, are friends who share a house and a cat. No disputes are caused by the house, but Plautus, the cat incites them to a rivalry for his favours. The portrait of Plautus stands alone in Compton-Burnett novels. He has been named, his owners explain, after Plautus, the Roman writer of plays, justifying the name by declaring that neither Plautus has written any good plays. In considering the plot of *Darkness and Day* it has been remarked that there is a moment when daylight breaks in and *Œdipus Rex* gives way to *A Comedy of Errors*. The last play was based on the *Menaechmi* of Plautus, so that, even if his productions were not of the highest literary merit, one of his themes was undeniably hard-wearing. Appropriately, Plautus the cat is the most hard-wearing character in *Mother and Son*, subduing even cat-hating Miss Burke, to whom his presence is the one drawback in a situation far more agreeable than the martyr's position offered by Miranda Hume.

As it happens, Miranda's post is filled by the instrumentality of Miss Burke. Her arrival at the home of Miss Greatheart and Miss Wolsey has coincided with the evaporation of the latter's income. Rather than be supported by her friend, Hester applies to be a companion to Mrs Hume, and, fortified by procedural hints from Miss Burke, finds herself engaged by letter. Rosebery, alone, is at home to greet Hester, and they have a cosy cup of tea together, all the sweeter, as Rosebery says, because the cup is unsweetened. Rosebery has explained that his mother continues to indulge him ' "with the generous lumps" ', though he has long lost his taste for such a sugary cup. Although he cannot bring himself to break to his mother that he has an outgrown childish love of sugar, Rosebery has made a more important decision. In his customary conversational chinoiserie, he confides to Hester that he expects his cousin Francis to succeed him, eventually, in his father's property. Rosebery brushes to one side any question of marriage for himself, which Hester raises after a suitable pause. Rosebery's disavowal has just been repeated, to contradict Hester's hint that many men have found themselves subject to a change of plan about their own celibacy, when Miranda returns with her family.

Although finding Hester promising material for companionship, Miranda makes it clear that this will not include the prospect of harpooning Rosebery as a husband. She has also some acid comments to make on Hester's tendency to encourage Tabbikins, the kitchen cat, who lacks Plautus's privileges. Tabbikins has, however, his own shrewd idea of tactics, and on a foray to the dining-room flatters Miranda into tolerating his presence by settling on her knee.

'"Are you proof against insult, Miss Wolsey?" said Francis "Because if not this is no place for you."

"Yes, that kind of insult, the natural antagonism of a woman in old age to one in her prime," said Hester, speaking easily and not looking at Julius.'

Actually Hester has already looked at Julius with an eye of sexual calculation, enabling her to accept without rancour Miranda's warning that Rosebery is devoted only to his mother. Julius is not, however, one of the party which goes to visit Hester's former home, a party led by Hester and consisting of Miranda and Rosebery. This is the first of three social occasions which mark the pattern of the book's plot, and precipitate its action.

Before the guests arrive Emma and Miss Burke arrange the luncheon, and how it is to be served to give a proper

impression of elegance without ostentation. Long association
with Plautus has given Miss Greatheart a feline touch of
her own. After agreeing that the unmended napkins should
be used, Emma Greatheart conveys to Miss Burke that the
previous housekeeper made time to mend the napkins that
developed holes. But Miss Burke makes it clear that she will
have no time to mend, and that, as neither Plautus nor Emma
are prepared to take up their needle, worn napkins are doomed
to be discarded.

As it happens, Miss Burke's stock rises throughout Mrs
Hume's visit, she being already impressed by the evidences
of the easy life that Emma and Hester have led together.
Plautus's untimely regurgitation of the half-consumed portion
of a mouse, does not abolish Miranda's respect for a household that takes coffee after dinner, and has a gardener in its
employment. Even Miss Burke's self-assertion in correcting
Rosebery when he says he cannot remember who had a
' "coward soul" ', does not hinder Miranda from congratulating Miss Burke on the excellence of the meal she has cooked.
Miranda's new-found respect for Miss Burke is increased by
her recognition that the latter has been wise to conceal her
domestic talents from such a task mistress as Miranda knows
herself to be.

On reaching home, Miranda declares this to have been
her last outing, as she has now to face the knowledge that
her heart is exhausted and may, at any moment, cease to beat.
Anything that has to be said should be said without delay
by her husband or by her son. Rosebery's life has no shadowed
corners, but, shaken by the news of his wife's precarious
state, Julius tells the secret that he feels must have been
suspected. When Rosebery, grown to manhood, began to
absorb all his mother's interest, Julius took a mistress, and
from this affair the three children were born. The coincidence
of a brother's death abroad has allowed Julius to bring up

the children as his nephews and niece. Uncharacteristically, this brief but fruitful liaison has escaped Miranda's notice. Without shame, she admits to peering into every corner of her household, but though she can detect the exact consumption by Mr Pettigrew and his pupils of the ' "plain cakes . . . that our custom assigns to the schoolroom" ' and sense the moment when she may surprise Julius and the children drinking wine she has forbidden him to give to them, she has overlooked her husband's sexual revolt. Her reception of the news is unsparing to Julius. Having quoted 'And all our yesterdays have lighted fools the way to dusty death', Miranda speaks her mind with hatred and contempt of the man who has deceived her in the past and undeceived her only when the future before her is brief. More brief, perhaps, than she expected, for, after a grudging word of forgiveness, Miranda hisses out that she thanks God she has not dealt with Julius as he has with her, and with these words expires.

This exit, as well as being dramatically effective, is well-timed for Julius and his children. The author was never one to shrink from dealing with the problems of moral pigeons coming home to roost, but the prospect of life among the Humes continuing, with Miranda's increased grudge against the children to poison the atmosphere, would be a horror better unexplored.

Hester has been within earshot throughout the scene, and uses the opportunity to strengthen her position as a necessary member of the household. It is Rosebery, shaken at losing a mother, and gaining two brothers and a sister, who breaks the news of Miranda's death to the children. In their difficulty of being respectful to Miranda's memory without telling obvious lies, Alice and Francis can only rejoice that words of comfort have been put into their mouths. Using a quotation that Compton-Burnett valued not only as a comment on grief, Alice remarks that Adrian's heart ' "has no bitterness to know" ', but if Adrian's heart is free from bitterness the shock of a death has carried him beyond his own control. He weeps, and then makes an all too public inquiry if Julius could marry Miss Wolsey. The implications are smoothed over by the grown-ups, but not to Adrian's satisfaction, even when Alice points out that the day of a wife's death is an unusual one for a betrothal. ' "And could there be such haste, when it would mean offering Rosebery as a step-child?" "You can talk in your clever way, but I still think what I said." '

Before the slightly retarded Adrian is proved to have a true perception of Hester's plans, another secret is uncovered. Rosebery comes upon a letter and a photograph. The letter is from a man who has written to Miranda long ago, agreeing that her son shall be passed off as the child of Julius, and provided for by a sum of money that shall be, apparently, Miranda's own. The photograph is of a man who in type resembles Rosebery, accounting for Rosebery's lack of re-semblance to Julius. This unattractive light on Miranda's dying vituperation of her husband has the effect of making Julius and Rosebery feel distinctly better about each other, even when they discover that Hester has, once again, been an eavesdropper. With an honesty which gives his laboured pomposity a kind of dignity, Rosebery announces that he will resign his position as Julius's legal heir, and live on the money which was bestowed on his mother by his real father. It will be remembered that, in *A Family and a Fortune*, Edgar Gaveston, carefully honest about death and marriage, says it may be possible that one kind of emotion predisposes the heart to another. Miranda is still unburied when Rosebery, shaken at the double loss of mother and father, offers himself as a husband to his mother's companion, whose engagement specifically excluded such a possibility. Playing for higher stakes, Hester manages her refusal so as to strengthen her position as housekeeper to Julius and his children. Her display of sympathy for all parties increases when the unhappy Mr Pettigrew has to complain of the levity that has overtaken his pupils since Miranda's death.

' "We conquered Pettigrew in unfair fight," said Alice. "And he followed our example." '

Making a major strategical error, Hester takes Julius and Rosebery to luncheon with Miss Greatheart. For this visit, which is a second turning point in *Mother and Son*, Emma and Miss Burke have another domestic conference in which Emma's feline qualities are again visible. Miss Burke remarks that Rosebery dislikes cats, and is perhaps afraid of them.

' "That is always why people do not like animals. I do not like bears and wolves myself."

"I believe I am afraid of Plautus."

"Yes, so do I, dear." '

While discussing the wine to be offered at luncheon, Miss Greatheart has admitted that she is proud that three people are coming to the meal, and that two of them are men. The men themselves might be less than proud and more than uneasy if they knew that Hester had passed on to her friend the news of her refusal of Rosebery, that Emma is aware of Hester's wish to marry Julius, and that Miss Burke has been informed of this interesting state of affairs. During the meal Julius finds Miss Greatheart's personality attractive, particularly when he learns that they have in common an unfinished novel reposing in a drawer.

(' "I wonder there is any drawer space left," said Miss Burke.')

The obvious harmony between Julius and Emma, and heavy gallantry from Rosebery towards Miss Burke, causes Hester to break up the party round the table. She has the nerve to add that she has never been in the position of the ignored single-ton when the company starts talking in pairs, but she has seen that Emma, although liking to the first person in Hester's own life is being far from repulsive towards Julius. For him, liberated from Miranda's unsympathetic domination, it is highly natural that he should be attacked by the complaint Compton-Burnett analysed in more than one of her novels, which might be called widower's rebound.

A third visit, when Emma and Miss Burke are to come to luncheon with the Humes, makes the children realise that Julius may be preparing to marry Miss Greatheart, and so give them an aunt. ' "And he knows what he does by giving us that." ' They go on to speculate what Miranda would think if Rosebery married Miss Burke, a step which he is, at that moment, arranging to take. Miss Burke accepts his offer, and they are able to have a cosy conspiratorial chat about Hester's fancy for Julius, and Julius's preference for Emma. Between this last pair matters have arranged themselves and the couples indulge in congratulations. Any awkwardness about what would have been Miranda's reaction is dealt with by Rosebery putting into the dead mouth ' "a cynical little speech" ' about life moving on even if one journey is at an end. Julius, with more complex feelings, says that it is no good to imagine Miranda saying anything else.

General goodwill is shattered by the entrance of Hester and the children, prepared for acting a charade. It is as a charade that Hester pretends to regard the engagements revealed to her. When their reality is insisted on, she snatches her knowledge of the family secrets like a pistol from a holster, and fires in all directions. Neither Julius nor Rosebery have yet told their prospective brides of the complications of parentage, until now concealed by Julius and by Miranda. Telling all she knows, Hester hastens to add the hope that Emma will not take the secret of Julius's past as hardly as did Miranda, whose death was precipitated by learning of his adultery. Even Hester does not blame Rosebery for the circumstances of his birth, but when he claims that Miss Burke is his first romance

Hester does not let his earlier proposal to herself pass unrecalled.

Having destroyed the fragile edifice in which her friends had hoped to live out their lives, Hester announces that she will now become a free traveller throughout the world. Her own edifice then collapses when Adrian, ever an asker of awkward questions, wants to know if she will be able to afford such a wide-ranging scheme of life. In the present emergency Hester can only disappear from the house, as Julius rightly insists that she should be separated from the children. Suddenly ceasing to be orphans, the children themselves have to sort out the goings-on of their elders with the help of historical examples.

' "Was Uncle like a man with a mistress in history?" [said Adrian]

"Yes," said Francis, "but when it is not in history, it seems to be different."

"And the man who was Rosebery's father, was the same?"

"Yes," said Alice, "but when the mistress is Aunt Miranda, it seems more different still." '

When Adrian continues his career of speaking words better unsaid by letting out the truth of his origins to Mr Pettigrew, Julius, Francis and Alice all reassure him by saying that at least it is a matter that cannot be mentioned to the family, and that Adrian may have only confirmed what has been long suspected in the neighbourhood.

Returning to Emma's house to say good-bye to Plautus, Hester is once more caught up in the easy companionship from which she might seem to have become an unforgivable outlaw. Plautus is the excuse that has brought Hester to the house for a farewell visit, and it is the attribution to Plautus of a cat's traditional dislike of moving house that gives Emma the excuse for breaking her engagement. Pleasure in flattery led her to accept Julius, with the understanding that she would be the second person in his life. Her discovery that, allowing for a wife, a mistress and three children, her place would be only sixth has dissuaded her from entering a state she has never honestly coveted. To Hester, Emma says, has come the reward of wickedness that has prospered. Between the friends it is decided that Hester can only display greatness of spirit, after showing so much littleness, by returning to accept the support her friend offers. An offer of support also solves the problem of retaining Miss Burke, who accepted Rosebery when she thought him to be Julius's son, and only continued the engagement from a base seeking for security. The prospect of a lifetime of ministering to the two friends, even with Plautus to plague her, appears like liberty compared with owing her support to one whom she has always addressed as Mr Rosebery, and who has never called her anything except Miss Burke, sharing with the reader an ignorance of her Christian name.

When Rosebery receives his dimissal from Miss Burke, he makes a brave attempt to persuade his father that he has himself, changed his mind. An attempt doomed to failure, for Julius has also received his congé from Miss Greatheart, who, unknown to the rejected suitors, has written both the letters, Miss Burke distrusting her own powers of exposition. The children receive this return to the status quo with pleasure unconcealed, though Francis mutters to Adrian that his brother should curb his rejoicing that Miranda will be absent from their lives. Ever an optimist, Rosebery tries to interest the children in games his mother taught him in his own childhood, but their lack of zeal increases his feeling of isolation. Moved by this melancholy sense of his superfluity, Rosebery announces that he has received a letter, sent by his real father, and that he will seek out this surviving parent, with whom he will make his home. (It is tempting to reconstruct the announcement which has caught the eye of Miranda's former lover, inciting him to write to Rosebery . . . 'suddenly, at home, in her eightieth year, Miranda, beloved wife of Julius Hume and devoted mother of Rosebery . . .'.) To their surprise, the children feel that the family circle will be too much reduced by Rosebery's departure, but almost immediately the scene changes from tragedy to farce Julius points out that the letter from Rosebery's father gives no address, although Rosebery assures the company that a voice they cannot hear will guide his steps.

' "Well, listen to the voice," said Julius, "and tell me where to send your letters . . ."

"He can't go now," said Adrian to Alice.

"No, he must stay here. It is the only address he knows." '

Mother and Son ends with no greater threat for the future than that of Rosebery, stranded like a whale in the children's schoolroom. The children have speculated as to whether the shocking pieces of news that Mrs Pettigrew receives from her husband will affect her delicate health, but the lightening flashes of scandal have at last passed from the landscape. Rosebery, kept apart by Miranda's vast selfishness, is now left companionless by her death, in spite of his moral qualities that even the children, while mocking him as 'Rosebud', can recognise.

In this study of companionship on several levels, the author treats it as a positive quality which can be separated from respect, and even from affection. It was the withdrawal of companionship from Julius, and its transfer to Rosebery, that drove Julius to console himself. By his extra-marital affair, he generated his own source of companionship, though the mother of his children, dying in Adrian's infancy, can have had little time to develop views on the subject. When the female household of Miss Greatheart settles down again, companionship is as much the reason of contentment as the security of Emma's income, in which of course Plautus has always had complete confidence. In considering *The Present and the Past*, it has been suggested that Cassius Clare wished to be thought of as a hero, and only approached that level by dying. With a success to be envied by many a Compton-Burnett tyrant, Plautus exacts the respect due to a god, but his habit of life makes him no hero. On the other hand Rosebery's transparent goodness of heart raises him above his sesquipedalian habits of speech and thought, almost to the point of being a heroic figure.

17

RESURRECTION HAS ITS
DIFFICULTIES

The death of Miranda Hume is also the death of the last of
Compton-Burnett's ravening matriarchs. It is true that in her
final, posthumously published, novel there is a second wife
who does her best to command her family, but she is not
accorded the kind of submission given to Miranda or to Sabine
Ponsonby (*Daughters and Sons*). In the next of her novels, *A
Father and His Fate* the author does indeed include one aspir-
ing matriarch, but Eliza Mowbray has to make do with a small
income and is frequently plagued by stirrings of rebellion.
Patriarchs, on the other hand, continue to appear in various
forms in the next four books. None of them control their
domestic empires with the extreme of repression achieved by
Duncan Edgeworth, but as their lapses from good behaviour
are due to licentiousness rather than miserly unkindness, they
are apt to be in a weaker moral position. This is no handicap
to their claims to be thought of as perfect beings.

Miles Mowbray, the father from whom *A Father and His
Fate* takes its title, has only three daughters in his family. His
estate is entailed on Malcolm, eldest son of his dead brother,
who has therefore been installed as the expectant heir in
Miles's household. Although she has the same Christian name
as the victimised Ellen Edgeworth (*A House and Its Head*),
Miles's wife, at the beginning of the story, has less to suffer,

186

and holds her own with ease. Perhaps this ease is too great for her husband's satisfaction, for, having failed to get the warm response from his daughters for which he had hoped, Miles says he can visualise that his wife's strength of character would lead her unflinching to the stake. According to Ursula, eldest and most cynical of his daughters, this prospect seems to offer some pleasure to her father. Constance, the next sister, makes difficulties for her family by nursing a moral courage which leads her towards religious mania, while Audrey, the youngest, is still pinned to the schoolroom under the supervision of Miss Gibbon. No one has had the cold-bloodedness to face the fact that, though Miss Gibbon's age has 'become stationary', Audrey's years continue to advance inexorably and now number nineteen.

In spite of warnings that to imitate King Lear is to risk meeting the same unsatisfactory reactions, Miles announces that a trial lies before his daughters and nephew. Family affairs, to inquire into which Miles and his wife are departing on a voyage, are in an even worse state than had been feared. By what economies, he asks, can his daughters suggest they could aid retrenchment? There is only a short silence at this inquiry, antithetical to King Lear's own inquisition, but made in the same spirit. Audrey suggests that, as her education has been unduly extended, other duties in the home might be found for Miss Gibbon. Constance offers to save the church organist's salary by taking on his job. Most pertinently, Ursula is prepared to organise her father's accounts, which do not appear to her to be on a sound basis; there is even a suggestion that some of Everard the butler's work could be undertaken by the daughters of the house. Malcolm, however, refuses to play his uncle's game, offering no more work than his present occupation of managing the estate.

' "My dear good girls!" said Miles, in a rather forced tone as if the scene had hardly reached his expectations ". . . Things are not as I said. Your father was playing King Lear again. . . ." ' Miles is faced with a more general disapproval than King Lear suffered for asking questions in the hope that the answers would boost his self-esteem. He is obliged to justify the false impression he has created, continue to employ Miss Gibbon for duties too nebulous to be defined, and, worst of all, stoop to placate the butler, who announces that if his services are deemed inessential, ' "I should hardly wish to stay where I am a fiasco." ' This threat is directed at Ellen, felt by Everard, not unreasonably, to be a more reliable authority than his master, and the conversation as to whether the cook might also be found superfluous proceeds in triangular fashion between Everard, Ellen and Miles.

From this scene of failed drama, Malcolm goes to visit his mother, Eliza, for whom his adopted family have feelings of fear, particularly Miles, and dislike, particularly Constance. Eliza plays her part of a beautiful woman, widowed and separated from her eldest son, with a zest undiminished by the isolation of her position, her sons giving her only the feelings she forces from them. Even Miss Manders, called Mandy, supposedly Eliza's companion, is more of a help and comfort to the boys than to their mother. In fact Eliza gives way to a burst of recrimination on the disloyalty of her household, when she overhears a discussion between Mandy and her sons on the difficulties that will face an expected newcomer.

This newcomer is Verena Gray, orphan daughter of a friend, and Eliza warns Malcolm and his younger brothers, Rudolf and Nigel, that Verena must be a sister to them, falling in love being prohibited by her poverty and their youth. Hardly has this warning been given when Malcolm leads in the newly arrived Verena, making it immediately clear that the warning was necessary, and that Malcolm will not heed it. Verena has 'wide blue eyes, straight features and a strong chin', a countenance very suitable for a girl who is orphaned but far from helpless. There is something of Florence Lacy (*Elders and Betters*) in Verena's character, with the addition of a stronger, more calculating, sexuality. However, before these traits can be revealed, the elder Mowbrays set out on their voyage, after a Compton-Burnett scene of agonising farewell, which makes the actual parting a positive relief.

With a determination to be in on everything that is reminiscent of Matilda Seaton (*A Family and A Fortune*), Eliza insists on bringing her sons and Verena to dinner. Her personality gets out of hand, after an attempt to be, simultaneously, the most important guest, the deputy hostess and the sympathetic aunt, Malcolm and Verena announce their engagement, and the only role left to Eliza is that of an over-possessive mother, disputing her son's plans to break away into matrimony. Malcolm remarks, aside to his cousin Audrey, that his mother cannot be a happy woman because she thinks she is a goddess and ' "must always be finding that people disagree" '.

Contrary to confident prediction, the news arrives that a shipwreck has befallen Miles and Ellen, and that Miles alone is the survivor. The sufferings of the family are increased by Constance insisting that she and her mother now stand together in knowing that death is not the end of life. Eliza adds to her intrusive commiserations a determination that Malcolm's brothers shall chaperon Verena in her walks with Malcolm.

' "She does not want my name coupled with Malcolm's," said Verena.

"You will soon be coupled with me yourself. So we need not consider that." '

Unusually explicit whether intentionally or not, in its physical implications, this statement is not, as a prophecy, immediately accurate. Verena, refusing to accept any domination from Eliza, has also declared that she likes older men.

Miles, Verena says, may find her of interest to him, and she speaks correctly. Returning with the proper sentiments of one recently widowed, Miles finds the first sight of Verena lifts up his heart. A private interview, when the acceptance of Verena as a fourth daughter is being sealed with a kiss, is interrupted by Eliza, bringing condolences already become otiose. Miles has been strongly attacked by widower's rebound, and rejects Eliza's attempts at a comforting session, when widowed heart should speak to widowed heart. Verena is a honey-pot, and Miles asks no more consolation than to drown in sweetness.

' "I think we did not quite realise what Father needed," said Constance.

"Neither did he, until he met it," said Malcolm.'

The family can only watch as Miles achieves a complete take-over of Verena, unheeding protests that his conduct is both heartless and grotesque. Verena relishes the devotion of the head of the family, and sees her way to an immediate position of power, instead of waiting, as Malcolm's wife and a guest in the house, until death shall remove Miles. When he announces his engagement to Verena, Miles has cast aside compunction to the point that he can insist that Malcolm should have no grouse at his fiancée changing her mind, while himself displaying complacency at the prospect of a new life with a young bride. Mandy, who has been the first to suspect Miles's interest in Verena, listens to a report from Rudolf and Nigel on this ill-assorted rearrangement of partners. Condemning Miles's behaviour towards his nephew, Miss Manders envisages, with a smile, the impossible idea that Ellen Mowbray might return to this shocking scene.

It turns out that Mandy has good reason to smile. Miss Gibbon's devotion to Ellen has always been recognised, as it stimulated the former governess's efforts to make a permanent place for herself in the Mowbrays' home. Now, while Miles is dwelling with pleasure on his future with Verena, Miss

Gibbon is observed behaving in a furtive manner over the disposal of Ellen's wardrobe. Miles comes upon a parcel and an addressed envelope, but though he makes a note of the address, his only overt reaction is to see that Miss Giddon is protected from inquiries about certain visits she makes to a friend. In the meantime Verena has come to sleep in the house, instead of making daily visits, an arrangement offensive to the taste of the day as compromising to a prospective bride, and seen with suspicion, later justified, by Miles's chronically shocked family.

Another shock now hits Ellen Mowbray's husband and daughters. Shaken by the news that the wedding of Miles and Verena will take place in a week's time, Miss Giddon breaks it to the girls that their mother, surviving the shipwreck in a state of collapse, has now returned to the neighbourhood in secret. She is waiting to re-enter her home until she has recovered her nerve, a wise precaution, it might be thought, for anyone proposing to resume life as the wife of Miles. This resurrection of a spouse brings on a family crisis, infinitely more painful than any embarrassment caused by the return of Fulbert in *Parents and Children*.

Overhearing this news, Verena cannot be expected to rejoice, but she shows both her youth and her tough egotism in making an impassioned appeal that Ellen should remain hidden. Miss Giddon has said that Ellen, still convalescent, hesitated to return when she heard that Miles planned to remarry. To Verena this appears a reason for letting Ellen remain dead. Having convinced herself that Miles is surrounded by a hostile set of Gonerils and Regans, she ignores both the legal points laid before her by Malcolm and Ellen's daughters' words that to abandon their mother would be the worst heartlessness. Miles, on hearing the news from Constance, puts up no display of joy. His wordless parting from Verena contains the hint that her frantic insistence that she still has the right to marry Miles may come from the growth of another secret.

Although Miles prays, in the actual words, that the cup may pass from him, Ellen comes back to her home. Eliza's welcome includes the news that Verena will now marry Malcolm, and Miles tenaciously insists that the young pair shall live under his roof, in spite of past and present objections that might be thought prohibitive to family peace. There remains, also, the mystery as to who has transmitted sums of money to Ellen during her exile, money for which Miss Gibbon has not been responsible. In the face of probing remarks from Constance, Miles is determined that the anonymity of the unknown donor should be respected, adding that he suspects that this may well be a woman. Miles then proceeds to sum up the troubles that have overtaken him and his courage in supporting them, likening his fortitude to that of people going to the scaffold and the stake, the latter destination having been earlier in his mind for a display of fortitude by Ellen. Miles complains that he did not have the help of the admiration usually extended to calm sufferers on their way to death, just a row of shocked faces and Eliza's sons ' "behaving as if they had come to gape at a spectacle" '. Miles is always sensitive to the vibrations of fascinated interest as to what their uncle will do next, which emanate from Nigel and Rudolf.

In greeting Malcolm and Verena on their return from their honeymoon, Miles's attitude is paternal, but Verena's is far from daughterly. One glance at Ellen tells her that she is faced with the most slippery of adversaries, an opponent fixed in kindly determination that passions shall be subject to good manners. Throughout tea Verena gives a display of bitchiness which, surrounded as she is by men who have liked her too much and women who hardly like her enough, makes her almost a figure of pathos. In its *genre* this passage is among Compton-Burnett's most accomplished, building up from

Verena's insistence that Miles should remember how she likes her tea, through her distaste for the rooms she is to share with Malcolm, to references to a time when she expected herself to be pouring out from the ceremonial silver teapot, and to be sharing a room with Miles. Finally, when Eliza and her younger sons have made their usual uninvited appearance, Miles becomes exasperated, and refers to the immediate past, when he hoped to marry Verena, as a ' "phantom time" '.
' "It did not seem to be," said Verena, looking into his face. "And we may find it was not." '

The threat in Verena's words is underlined by Eliza's announcement that she expects to become a grandmother, to her the most important aspect of her son's wife's pregnancy. At this point, Verena's harping on her past with Miles forces Ellen to tell her husband's one-time fiancée that, for the sake of all their lives together, the past must seem to be forgotten. When Malcolm adds his weight to his aunt's request for an act of oblivion, Verena, brooding amid the general hostility, says that she would make the effort to accept and appreciate Ellen, if she could only demonstrate that Ellen herself shared the pains of rejection.

Verena's opportunity arises through a lapse by Miles in covering his tracks. As the money sent anonymously to Ellen has ceased to arrive it is obvious that whoever sent it is aware that it is no longer needed. Miles has overlooked the fact that Verena has seen him hiding a registered envelope addressed to Ellen, an envelope unused because of Ellen's return. Making her last assault on the reunion of Ellen and Miles, Verena finds a pretext for fetching some registered envelopes from Miles's desk and laying them on the family breakfast table, where conversation still hovers about the identity of Ellen's benefactor.
' "Give the envelopes to me," said Miles, holding out his hand, with his eyes on them.

"It is Malcolm who wants them. I hope I have brought enough." She had brought one too many.'

Although Miles is now revealed as having been aware that his wife was alive when he planned remarriage, he puts up a cloud of obfuscation, under the grilling in which his daughter Constance is grand inquisitor. The envelope which has betrayed Miles is at length passed to Constance to destroy, and with a final touch of ineffability, Miles hands the money it has contained to Ellen, though in fairness it is hard to know to whom else the money is owed. Verena has had her revenge, but as Ursula says, ' ". . . revenge, like other things, may be best in anticipation" '.

Eliza, inevitably, appears, the power to keep away, as her son Malcolm says, having been left out of her. Her attempts to catch up with the complications that have arisen are met by a counter-blast from Miles, on the grounds that Eliza's behaviour is insufferable, uncharitable, and generally inferior to his own, in spite of moments of error. He has hardly finished his tirade when Verena enters dressed for departure. She announces that she is leaving for ever, though she will return her child to be brought up by Malcolm and Ursula, who she suggests—her love of government ever strong— would do well to marry. In a private farewell to Miles, Verena reminds him that the child, which will be her memorial among the Mowbrays, will be his and hers.

Miles has always railed against the demeanour of Rudolf and Nigel, a justified distrust, for it is by a combination of their ubiquity and his own vanity that their uncle's gravest lapse is revealed beyond a select group of Ellen, Ursula, Malcolm and Miss Gibbon, who are already aware of the parentage of Verena's child.

Miss Gibbon asks for help to put some unwanted clothes into the top drawers of a chest in the bedroom of Miles and Ellen, this piece of furniture having been built for a giant ancestor. Eliza offers the assistance of her younger sons, she and Constance both suggesting that they have outstripped Miles in their growth. Annoyed by this insinuation, Miles demonstrates his superior height by removing some clothes which, unexpectedly, are already in the topmost drawer. Laid out before the eyes of Miss Gibbon and the boys, these clothes are seen to have been worn, and to be night clothes from Verena's trousseau. The evidence that he has been sleeping with Verena, knowing that their marriage will be prevented by Ellen's return, does not hinder Miles from greeting Rudolf's promise of secrecy not as male solidarity but as an insult. To betray this secret, Miles says, would be an infamy hardly human, an idea unfit to be mentioned before Miss Gibbon, and the boys are not to say that there is something else unfit for her.

' "Do you hear me?"

"Other people will if you are not careful," said Nigel.'

The two brothers return to Miss Manders with this burden of secrecy weighing on them, but they find relief in agreeing that the burden is intolerable, and their duty to tell everything to Mandy is older and more to be regarded than any promise to their uncle. At the end of the book Eliza is alone in having no suspicion that Miles is the father of Verena's child. The last word is Mandy's, hastening to agree with Eliza that Miles's promise to take a special care of Verena's daughter may be due to a fear that he might treat the child differently from the grandchildren for whom he is hoping.

The undercurrents in *A Father and His Fate* give it one of the most intricate plots of any Compton-Burnett novel. Miles might be said to be a Lear who is not only able to choose his own Cordelia, but to seduce her. Verena's power over him is increased by her genuine feeling that his family is heartless, and Miles enjoys her incitement to use his financial hold over his daughters to crush criticism of his plan to replace their mother by Verena. This disagreeable shaking of his stick of power, over daughters who have had no opportunity to be anything but dependent, deprives him of the sort of sympathy which the reader never loses for Sir Godfrey Haslam (*Men and Wives*). Verena herself is a perfect study of a female tyrant in embryo, and it must be felt that her daughter has had a lucky escape from being brought up by such a mother. The secret of the child's birth is known to so many of the bystanders that the ticking of this time-bomb will be audible to more people than is the case with some of the delayed action devices, which the author liked to leave on the last few pages of her novels.

If there is some weakness in the lines of character demarcation in *A Father and His Fate*—the voices of Ursula and Audrey strike the same note, as do those of Rudolf and Nigel—the book is strong on quotations which hit the bulls-eye. At her first appearance Verena quotes from Browning's *Grammarian's Funeral*, and Eliza recognises that such intellectual spryness signifies the newcomer's formidable character. In the last pages of the book Miles finds words coming into his mouth about his home, where he was ' "born, bred, looks to die" '. Constance's officious remark that her father is quoting is, at first, denied. Then Miles admits that he and the poet might well have had the same idea, but Constance remorselessly points out that the lines were written by a woman. Still maintaining that he has not quoted anyone, Miles adds that neither he, nor indeed any man, would quote a woman. Nor, he says, would any woman.

' ". . . the poet was Christina Rossetti, Father," said Constance.

"Rossetti was a man," said Miles, in a manner of meeting success himself.

"Christina was his sister."

"Oh, he had a sister? Well, that was different. I suppose it ran in the family. That proves what I said." '

With such an ability to put himself in the right in the face of evidence to the contrary, it is not surprising that Miles can surmount a shattering sequence of exposures. He regains his grip on his family, and they, like Rosebery Hume (*Mother and Son*) know no other address to which they can go. As in so many of Compton-Burnett novels, power is the quality most admired, and, except when death intervenes, the most rewarded. The slaves may revolt, their opportunities for liberty may seem glorious, but only too often the last sound in the reader's ear is the clanking of the chains of family subservience.

18

A TYRANT TAKES SHAPE

At the beginning of A *Heritage and Its History*, Simon
Challoner, a young man in his twenties, is the impatient and
expectant heir to his uncle's estate, with his father's life, as
well as his uncle's, between him and his heritage. At the end
of the book he has succeeded to the estate, but he is now a
middle-aged man, and his frustration has caused him to
develop into a particularly disagreeable parental bully. It is an
added bitterness in Simon's cup that his frustration has been
brought on himself by an incident of sexual abandon on his
part, an act unwarmed by any deep feeling. The book opens
with one of those breakfasts which are prolonged until it
overlaps into the preparations for luncheon. Against this
background, Simon sets out his self-pitying complaint to
Walter, his younger brother. Loving the house and the estate
with a passion greater even than his devotion to his brother,
Simon can only see a prospective wife and her children as a
consort and descendants. The barrier before which Simon
fumes is composed of his uncle, Sir Edwin Challoner, a robust
sixty-nine, and Simon's father Hamish, who, though the
younger of this elder devoted pair of brothers, is observed to be
in fading health. Julia, wife of Hamish, is supported by a
strong religious faith, not only at the prospect of losing her
husband, but in the realisation that Sir Edwin has superseded
her in her husband's heart. She has also to attempt to subdue

Simon's open calculations as to how soon he may expect to come into his kingdom, while coping with Walter's decision to abandon his career at Oxford in favour of writing less than minor poetry. Julia's only ally in the house is Deakin, the kindliest of Compton-Burnett butlers, whose regard for his mistress is increased by her lack of attention to the minutiae of domestic affairs.

In this first chapter, Walter's character becomes fixed in the shape of one who has retreated to the side-lines of life, in the same mood as he has retreated from the university. His bills and his poems he has destroyed together, with the confidence that even if the poems are not reborn, the bills will, on their reappearance, be paid by his mother. As Julia's son Simon says, she likes to be trusted, and so, by laying his bills on her table, Walter is glad to cause her pleasure by giving her his full trust. Simon has none of the resignation which leads Walter to settle down as a *raisonneur*. He finds it impossible to keep off the subject of what is to him a view from Pisgah, though Moses did not have to complain of an overgrowth of creeper, which darkens the house that is the centre of Simon's Promised Land.

Hamish's increasing weakness makes his progress ever slower, when Sir Edwin escorts his brother to tea with Rhoda and Fanny Graham. It is the day of Rhoda's thirty-eighth birthday, Fanny being twelve years younger, but Hamish's decay casts a gloom, increased by Sir Edwin's brooding on the future. He feels enough sympathy with Rhoda to ask if he may count on her friendship when he loses his brother, ungallantly admitting that her friendship would be a meagre substitute for life lived with Hamish. More cheerfully, Hamish himself talks of the future which he will not share, which, he says, has to him the lightness of interest of a picture or a play. (The dramatisation of A *Heritage and Its History* does not, as it happens bring Hamish on to the stage, though it is his death which precipitates the dramatic situation.) When Simon and Walter have joined the party with the object of helping their father home, there is an edginess in the conversation which leaves the spinster sisters in a disturbed state. Both are conscious that Rhoda has been singled out by Sir Edwin, but their verbal duel is limited to contradicting each other about the characters of Walter and Simon. Speaking more truly than she then knows, Rhoda says that Simon seems rather heartless to her, but with a tolerance that will be useful to her later, Fanny defends him as only more honest than most men.

Both Simon's honesty and his lack of heart emerges unmodified at his father's death. Immediately he struggles to effect a series of petty changes, from the alteration of his father's system of keeping the rent schedules, to the removal of a bookcase, to him scarcely less objectionable than the offending creeper in its obliteration of the daylight. Seeking to check these irreverent suggestions, Julia can only take the extreme, and ignored, step of ordering her grown-up son out of the room. The futility of this proceeding, and the bickering among the surviving members of his family, impresses on Sir Edwin an ever-deeper sense of his isolation. In a grief-stricken huff, he goes to seek, at the house of the Graham sisters, something to make up for his loss.

This compensatory friendship takes an unexpected turn, when Sir Edwin announces that he will be married to Rhoda Graham on the following day. Beyond saying that the room next to his will be prepared for his bride, he vouchsafes no information, and forbids any questions on the subject. Knocked down like skittles by this news, it takes the family an appreciable time to recover enough breath for congratulation. Remaining inimitably himself, Simon hurries out a question as to whether his uncle thinks of having a family, and, although receiving a snub, assumes that Sir Edwin has implied what Simon wishes to hear.

' "I suppose it is to be a formal marriage," said Simon, ". . . there are to be two rooms. I think we can be sure of our ground there. . . . we shall be more dependent on [my mother's] income, with the demand for Rhoda's widowhood." '

As Walter points out, that, although Simon seems only to conceive of Rhoda as a widow, it is not as a widow that she will begin her married life. In her new character as Lady Challoner, Rhoda is only anxious not to disturb a household long set in its own practices. Simon is drawn by this warmhearted pliability, perhaps finding Rhoda's sympathy a change from his mother's despairing appeals that he should modify his bare-faced calculation. At some moment, not defined, calculation is forgotten and self-control is lost, with the result that Simon finds himself obliged to break to Walter that Rhoda is with child by him. Paradoxically, any deception is impossible, because Simon's earnest hope that his uncle's marriage would be 'formal' has been fulfilled.

It is not the purpose of this study to examine reviews of Compton-Burnett's books, but it would be fair to mention that, in 1959, when A Heritage and Its History first appeared, Simon's seduction of Rhoda was considered, by more than one critic, to be incredible, if not impossible. It was objected that Rhoda's greater age, and Simon's obsession with his inheritance, would have inhibited such a union. Against these objections, it would be well to remember, yet again, the words of Edgar Gaveston (A Family and A Fortune) that emotion of one kind may dispose the mind to another. Hamish's death has left Simon still an expectant heir, and not an inheritor. Rhoda's marriage has given her only the outward semblance of a wife. Simon's life has changed too little, Rhoda's has changed too much. Consequently the slightly conspiratorial friendship which they share has a result out of all proportion to their feelings for each other. When Grant Edgeworth (A House and

Its Head) seduces Alison, the bride of Duncan, his uncle, and by this means disinherits himself, it is the action of a practised womaniser, responding to the appeal of a beautiful newcomer. Simon's behaviour appears to be the result of inexperience, stimulated by brooding on the sexual implications of his uncle's marriage. As Rhoda says, later in the novel when the secret can be kept no longer, ' "What Simon and I did is done in all days." '

Julia, in no one's confidence, is baffled by the lack of rapture at the advent of a child, but as Rhoda and Simon let their friendship fade, she has no suspicion that there have been frightening scenes between Rhoda and her husband, and between Simon and his uncle. Sir Edwin, unlike Duncan Edgeworth (A *House and Its Head*), does not strike in the face the nephew who has deceived him, but in an analogous situation he takes a more subtle revenge. When the son, another Hamish, is born Sir Edwin accepts the child as his heir, and Simon is faced with disinheritance brought about by his own action. (The reader is told that Simon's 'blindness to his coming displacement was the only error he never confessed to his brother'.) Sir Edwin remarks, with sadistic cheerfulness, that in any case Simon's son would have come after his father, and that this foreshortening of the future only means that Simon's life has been cut out of the succession. Simon does not find it easy to contemplate the cutting out of his own life, fond as he has been of the thought of cutting off the lives of his elders. With a relenting, that is also a twisting of the knife in Simon's wound, Sir Edwin offers Simon the post of agent, administrator where he had hoped to be inheritor, with the proviso that both his nephews and their mother should set up a separate home.

During Rhoda's pregnancy, Simon has been making a friend of her sister Fanny. He solves the problem of finding a new home by proposing to her, with the assurance to his

family that Fanny seeks marriage rather than romance, and
that he will take care to be a good husband. Walter finds the
move to be no wrench, except that he suffers for Simon, who
goes with melancholy into exile. Deakin, the butler, suffers
for the loss of Julia, while Julia happily looks forward to the
prospect of grandchildren. Already this prospect begins to
cast a shadow, when there chances to be talk that a daughter
of Simon and Fanny would, as a close cousin, be an undesirable match for Sir Edwin's supposed son, Hamish.

' "It was like a Greek tragedy," said Walter, "with people
saying things with a meaning they did not know, or with
more meaning than they knew." '

Twenty years later there was a farcical entr'acte between the
first and last scenes of the Greek tragedy. Simon is now the
harassed father of five children. His occupation as agent to
his uncle keeps his lost heritage ever before his eyes, while it
does not keep him sufficiently busy to exhaust his energies.
From this superfluity of time on their father's hands his elder
children are the sufferers, with no escape from Simon's constant nagging except that they still have meals of economical
dreariness, ' "organised rigour" ', upstairs on the nursery
floor. At this moment Graham is eighteen, Naomi and Ralph
a year and two years younger. Claud and Emma are after-
thoughts of three and two years old, too young as yet to come
under the blight spread by Simon, when he considers the
painful difference between the prospects of his legitimate
children, and those of his elder, but unacknowledged, son
Hamish. This boy has passed from Eton to Oxford, while
Graham and Ralph are coached privately and economically
for their university entrance examination, their father perpetually harping on the theme that success at Oxford is all
that stands between them and the workhouse. Once again
Simon is seen to have arranged his own discomfiture. The
threat of the workhouse becomes, in the hands of his children,

a sharp weapon of mockery, making Simon's reiteration of its imminence appear both sour and absurd.

The luncheon party which celebrates Sir Edwin's eighty-ninth birthday gives an opportunity for this jest to be played with among the younger guests. The years of concealment have encouraged Rhoda in a tendency to gush, which is mimicked by her nephew Ralph. ' "Ah, how we say it for you," murmured Ralph . . . "And how we all mean it! Ah, how we do!" '

Simon's request to have this mimicry repeated to him is only the first of a sequence of nagging criticisms of his sons, which ultimately goads Ralph into telling his father that he should be ashamed of working off his own disappointment by blaming his children for the bleakness of their future prospects. ' "I hope father will drop dead on his way home," said Ralph. "I really do hope it. I don't know how I am to meet him. And we could repair to the workhouse. It has come to seem homelike." '

Simon, however, survives, to face the feared complication of Hamish and Naomi falling in love, of which there has already been a hint at the birthday luncheon party. Four years later, through a closed door, Emma and Claud overhear an exchange of marriage plans between Hamish and Naomi, and their tearful grief at the idea of this pre-emption of their sister attracts their father's attention. Simon is reduced to silence at the hideous implications of what his children have overheard. Even his shrunken heart has warmth for Naomi, who has an attractive intelligence, and none of the morbidity which darkens the life of Lavinia Middleton, to be met with in a somewhat similar situation in The Mighty and Their Fall.

At the moment all Simon can do is to tell Claud and Emma that Hamish and Naomi are too nearly related by blood to marry. His discomfiture might have been increased, if that were possible, had he heard his youngest children's con-

clusions when he has left them. Claud sums up the difficulties
he sees ahead by saying that he now realises that he and
Emma will have to wait to marry until they are too old to
have to heed their father's prohibition, or, as Simon's daughter
says, ' ". . . until he is too old to understand." '

The climax of the Greek tragedy has now to be faced by
Sir Edwin, Rhoda and Simon. This unexpectedly united front
is baffling to Julia and Fanny, who are in favour of a marriage
that, except for the pair being first cousins once removed,
seems to be all that could be desired. Supported by the
sympathy of her mother and her grandmother, Naomi holds
her ground. She stands firm in the face of her father's appeal
to trust his superior knowledge, Sir Edwin's threat to disinherit Hamish, and a more subtle attack, because of its
unexpectedness, in which Walter urges the moral dignity to
be won by renunciation. Walter carries the news that Hamish
and Naomi are resolute, and Rhoda makes one last attempt
to hold up the roof of dissimulation under which the young
people have lived. She begs that concealment should continue,
the risk of genetic ill-effects being remote, but she is beaten
by the combination of her husband and her nephew by
marriage who is the father of her son. She tells her husband
that she will never think quite the same of him again, to
which he replies that such a moment arises in most human
relationships; it came to Sir Edwin himself regarding Rhoda,
but he is more fortunate as his downfall has come when his
life is nearly over.

The reader has seen Simon grow into a petty carping tyrant,
unable to come to terms with the result of his own lapse. He
has now to face a circle of judges who have been the sufferers
from his sickness of heart. When the situation has been
explained in all its crudity, Simon asks for Ralph's opinion,
and has to stomach the reply that Ralph has thought his father
' "hard and self-righteous; and now I feel that you were both

and should have been neither."' As Fanny says, when Simon asks for opinions he can hardly expect not to hear them.

Unable to face the problems of his inheritance, Hamish struggles to emerge from his state of double shock by saying that he must travel away from Naomi, and that he will resign what should be Simon's heritage. Not unreasonably determined that the façade of decorum shall not collapse, Sir Edwin vetoes any renunciation. Privately, however, Hamish insists to Simon that he will restore the property to his father, the legal heir, but with more understanding of this son's character than he has shown towards his legitimate children, Simon says he will welcome and expect a retraction of this offer.

The revelations have been less startling than those in *Darkness and Day*, but when Walter is left alone with his nephews and niece there is the same mental struggle to regain balance on ground which has suddenly lost its shape. Walter has wished he were Shakespeare to do justice to the scene that has passed, and Graham adumbrates that they must all wish they were something else. The family life has been built on a basis of fear of Simon, and now that he has been toppled there is a blank. Hamish, at least, as Ralph points out, has escaped twenty-four years of being Simon's son. In spite of Simon's warnings, the idea that the heritage may change its course begins to seep through the household, and though Simon denies speculation about riches from the younger children, he relaxes his economies sufficiently to allow them to buy a book at the village Post Office. The children's nurse has passed on the rumour about a change from poverty, which suggests that eavesdropping may be playing its customary domestic role.

As Sir Edwin begins to feel that death is coming nearer, the time spent waiting for Hamish's return is filled by a series of farewells, in which Emma and Claud behave with tact and dignity. Simon gets a set-down when he tries to enforce Julia's suggestion that the children might kiss their great-uncle's hand. They say that this command is not reasonable as he is not prepared to set them such an example. Sir Edwin himself gives a final jab at Simon, by remarking that the jokes about the workhouse, never suppressed in spite of frenzied prohibitions, have been an amusement of his old age. On Hamish's arrival, Sir Edwin lays a last command on him that he will not evade the burden of his inheritance, and while Simon acquiesces in yet another dashing of the cup from his lips, the rest of the family prick up their ears on hearing Hamish say he will not be without support in his new duties. Hamish, as Graham says, has suffered a sea-change, which, it transpires after Sir Edwin's funeral, has been wrought by an engagement to marry. There is a general sense of outrage that Hamish should have found a new love, though it is felt that Simon goes rather far in suggesting to Naomi that they are fellow-sufferers, she from losing her first love, he from losing, once again, his estate.

Hamish has prepared his family for a formidable bride, some years older than himself, and if anything he has understated the strength of her personality. Marcia takes one look round the house, and decides that such haunted spaciousness is no background for the life she plans to lead with Hamish. Simon, for his part, takes one look at Marcia and is smitten by a *coup de foudre*. Her own feelings are aroused to an extent visible to Simon's wife and Hamish's mother, both with experience of Simon's powers of attraction. Marcia proposes that Hamish's earlier promise of resigning his heritage should be made good, creating a yet stronger feeling of sympathy between herself and Simon. In this highly charged atmosphere, it is agreed that Marcia and Hamish should take Rhoda and make a home together at a distance from Simon, no one being prepared to face the risk that Simon might be tempted, once again, to breed himself out of his heritage.

Basking in the glow of being restored to his old home, Simon joins in a family discussion about the character of Marcia, speaking as more of an authority on the subject than his acquaintance with her would seem to justify. This leads to a comment from Ralph that there is a photograph of Marcia, a good likeness, which has been removed from the hall to Simon's private study. It is not a habit of the family to display photographs, and Fanny gets in a wifely dig that this one will now be seen by Simon alone. Ralph presses on to inquire as to what made Marcia present the photograph in the first instance, and Naomi, in exasperation, blocks further comment.

' "She did not think of it. Father asked for [the photograph]," murmured Naomi. "Will you ever stop pursuing the truth?" ' Oaths find no place in Compton-Burnett dialogue, but at the end of this aside of Naomi's, as she represses her brother's denseness, the words 'You bloody fool,' seem almost to form themselves on the page.

Walter, who knows how the loss of an inheritance can destroy a character, begins to speculate that a son of Hamish and Marcia's, finding himself a landless baronet, might feel, resentfully, that an eldest son's eldest son should have precedence rising above bastardy. The possibility of such troubles is cancelled by the arrival of telegrams telling of Hamish's grave illness and then of his death, with words added to say that Marcia is not pregnant. Even at the moment of his eldest son's death, Simon can comment on Marcia's consideration in saving Simon from the fear that he might have to wait for months until the sex of an unborn child had declared itself, and he can at last enjoy his heritage in its entirety.

Family rearrangements include the return of Rhoda and Marcia to a nearby house, there to live in biblical style as mother-in-law and daughter-in-law, like an earlier Naomi and the widowed Ruth. When this has been settled, Claud and Emma bring a wreath they have made in memory of Hamish, mentioning that he might have been their brother, indeed that people have said that he was. Perhaps relieved that to the children this means a possible relationship through marriage with Naomi, Simon rashly asks them how their lessons are going, and gets an undesired example of Emma's progress in the reading of hand-writing. Emma reads aloud a letter from Marcia to Simon, claiming that Hamish's death will still leave a bond between them. The book comes to an end amid a plethora of Ladies Challoner, Rhoda, Marcia and Fanny, two of them having borne Simon's children, and the third being destined, only too clearly, to be his mistress. But as Naomi points out, when Ralph fears that Simon's euphoria may die away and leave his life empty, preoccupation with Marcia will avert the perils of ennui. In the end it is Simon who orders the retention of the creeper on the house, a growth he had found so depressing when he was chafing at his dependence. Light, says Simon, might be too startling. As his brother Walter says when Simon's secret is first revealed, Simon is the hero of the tragedy, but it is a pity that he is the villain as well.

An element in the success of the dramatisation of *An Heritage and Its History* was the manageable number of its characters. Compared to some of Compton-Burnett's more densely populated novels the field might be called limited, with the minor characters such as the butler and the nurse giving only marginal aid in the development of the story. Throughout the book there are, however moments of gaiety among the younger generation, which lightens the gloom induced by Simon. In the novel that followed, *The Mighty and Their Fall*, which deals again with a father's temptations, the gloom is deeper and the highlights are flickering rather than sparkling.

19

INCEST IN THE MIND

The Mighty and Their Fall starts with a contest for access to a downstairs cloakroom, between Agnes Middleton, a coolly calculating girl of fourteen, and her brother and sister, Hengist and Leah, aged eleven and ten. Washing arrangements play little part in the country houses built by Compton-Burnett, but on this occasion the order in which the cloakroom is to be used is dictated by Lavinia, the elder sister of the children, who thus demonstrates her position as one of the Mighty. After her mother's death, this girl of twenty has grown to be a companion, almost a wife, to Ninian her father. Her concentration on him of all her powers of loving include such public demonstrations as holding hands at the family dinner table. There is also general assent that her time should be dedicated to helping her father in the management of an estate suffering from the anaemia that chronically debilitates the land of Compton-Burnett gentry.

Egbert, Lavinia's elder brother, has his own devotion to her, but is not in competition with their father. A more singular and suppressed affection is that of Hugo Middleton, a man of mysterious origins, adopted as a son by Ninian's father, and accepted as an uncle by Ninian's children. Uncles are apt to be the eunuchs in Compton-Burnett families, their situation recalling the explanation by the wife of the Victorian Archbishop Benson, when required to tell her band of brilliant children the difference between a bull and an ox. The bull, Mrs Benson said, was the father, and the ox was the uncle. Hugo Middleton makes an attempt to shake off the ox-like role in the course of *The Mighty and Their Fall*, but has no more success than Dudley Gaveston (*A Family and a Fortune*). Hugo is lucky, however, in being loved by Selina, Ninian's mother, as though he were her real son. Selina does her best to rule her family, but she faces a constant rebellion and accepts it with a resignation which Sabine Ponsonby (*Daughters and Sons*) would have despised. When she hears that the younger children are to eat in the dining-room, because the schoolroom ceiling is being repaired Sabine's only wonder is how the children managed to damage such an inaccessible surface, assuming without question that they must be responsible. Although exasperated by Miss Starkie, the governess's, self-satisfaction, Selina endeavours to bring home a sense of sin to Hengist and Leah, when they are detected in walking on a tag of wool depending from Miss Starkie's dress, and so assisting a further unravelling. The children are able to defeat their grandmother's assertion that there was ' "Someone Who Knew" '. They point out that if God sees everything he cannot, in a way, see anything.

God, of course, must be aware of the threat of brooding change hanging over the house, but He will also see its cause, unlike Ainger the butler who supposes that Hugo Middleton might be on the point of marriage. On the other hand Cook, so referred to throughout the book, discounts this idea, and it is, in fact, Ninian who announces his approaching wedding. Congratulations tail away into embarrassment when Lavinia's position, deprived of the object of her love and the occupation of her days, becomes painfully clear. The arrival of Teresa Chilton, Ninian's betrothed, to inspect her future family only makes Lavinia's state of desolation more obvious. Hugo, as he tells Teresa in a private interview, is prevented by lack of means from rescuing Lavinia by becoming more than an uncle to her, and in reply, Teresa, victim of a sudden fancy for Hugo, confides that she would be prepared for Hugo to be more than a brother-in-law to her.

In these circumstances it is hardly surprising that Teresa writes to tell Ninian that she cannot bring herself to marry him, because he offers her both too much in his family, and too little in himself. Ninian is far from pleased, and in addition his mother's journey up the stairs to the children, in order to tell of the breaking of the engagement, induces an illness, which well may be the last for Selina in her later eighties. At a moment when her grandmother's recovery seems almost impossible, Lavinia sorts the incoming post, which is her usual duty. The reader, alone is aware that she has suppressed one letter addressed to her father. There has, as it happens, been a miscalculation about Selina's recuperative powers, and her first step towards normal life is to examine the letters that have accumulated. Among them Selina finds a letter from Teresa (who has failed to persuade Hugo to propose to her). Teresa's letter tells Ninian that she would, after all, be prepared to marry him. There seems to be no explanation as to how the letter has been diverted, but as the time limit set by Teresa for a reply has not expired, the marriage, at last, takes place.

After the marriage, Teresa loses both her impetus as a character and her importance in a story which takes on an ever darker tone. The shadows begin to thicken when Selina's second and favourite son Ransom, announces that he is returning to see his mother before his own death. His mortal illness, he writes, is the result of 'wild oats', but anyone hoping for detailed symptoms of general paralysis of the insane will be disappointed. Shedding tears of joy at this return of a lost sheep, Selina takes a handkerchief handed to her by Lavinia, and in the transfer an envelope falls from her

granddaughter's pocket. It is the envelope of the letter from
Teresa to Ninian. Lavinia is shown not only to have suppressed the letter so that Teresa will think that she has been
rejected, but Lavinia, calculating on her grandmother's death,
has also planted the letter so that her family will deduce that
Selina has committed this mean action. Although suspecting
that the stratagem is Lavinia's, Selina's grandmotherly love
has been stronger than her desire for self-vindication, and
she has let matters lie unexplained. Selina is rewarded, for
when Ninian is unctuously offering Lavinia forgiveness without oblivion, Ransom, the long-absent son, makes a dramatic
entry.

Ransom, to whom Miss Starkie has given a résumé of the
situation, at once offers to take Lavinia away from a home
where she is under a cloud. He has set up a house of his own
in the neighbourhood, and he underlines his position as a
newly arrived benefactor by telling Ninian that Ranson's
own death will give a fortune to his brother.

' "What a day it has been!" said Hugo. "There is material
for an epic. The fall of Lavinia; the return of Ransom; the
uplift of Ninian; the tragedy of Ransom; the escape of Lavinia;
the lament of Selina. I hope there will be no more." '

On that day there is only, in addition, the words of Miss
Starkie, who associates herself with a disconcerted Ninian as
two guides who have contributed to Lavinia's fall by a failure
to impart moral standards. But soon afterwards another fall
is added to Hugo's epic. The humiliation of Ninian takes
place, which would be a fit addition to what might be a series
of allegorical paintings. Ransom has refused to satisfy Hugo
as to how he made his fortune, beyond the sinister words that
it was by ways accepted in their time and place, but he uses
the fortune itself to demonstrate that Ninian is no stronger
than Lavinia when faced with temptation. Sent to burn the
earlier of two wills, Ninian falls and burns the later one,

which would make Lavinia the heiress of Ransom's fortune. Ninian has been so exalted by the prospect of this money that he has come to regard it as his by right. Caught in the trap his brother has set, Ninian struggles verbally until he reaches the point that he can equate his own lapse with Lavinia's, and insist that Ransom's stratagem is of a baseness that neither he nor his daughter would have contemplated. He can even suggest that the eavesdropping, inadvertent but complete, by which Egbert and Hugo discover the Fall of Ninian, to be more reprehensible than the fall itself.

Ranson passes from the story, and the world, with words of warning to Lavinia that she should guard the fortune that will now be hers. Ransom's words are prophetic, for if, when caught out in burning the wrong will, Ninian was prepared to agree that Lavinia should be Ransom's heiress, his acquiescence changes to voracity when his brother is no more there to fight him on equal terms. Still exalted by the idea of relief from the money troubles of his estate, Ninian only pays heed to Lavinia's determination to keep her inheritance when she announces that she will be marrying a poor man. The poor man of her choice is her adopted uncle Hugo, and protests from Ninian, and from the outraged Miss Starkie, make no impression on the engaged couple. It rests with Selina to play, as it were, a stop card by announcing that Hugo is really her husband's son, and so a marriage between himself and Lavinia would come within the prohibited degrees. This union cannot be given the tacit acceptance that has allowed Ninian to develop an incestuously emotional relationship with Lavinia.

Outside the door, Ainger and Cook listen enthralled to the murky revelations, though the latter gives a nervous start when they are surprised by the pantry-boy, né Percival but rechristened James for professional convenience. Cook does not, however, slacken in retort to Ainger when he remarks that a governess is not what he would choose to be.

' "Well, the choice might not fall on you, Ainger. You might be seen as lacking in some points." '

Exasperated by the troubles his remarriage has brought on him, Ninian develops some of the characteristics which made breakfast with Duncan Edgeworth (A *House and Its Head*) such a scarifying ordeal. His mood gets blacker when Teresa, a complete failure as a sympathetic wife, points out that Hugo has returned from his search to establish the truth about his paternity. His early arrival has drawn the rest of the family out on the lawn to hear his news, and Ninian can only vent his annoyance by snubbing Ainger's suggestion that Hugo, after a night journey, might need a hot breakfast. Even without this support, Hugo is exhilarated by having discovered that his origins have been kept as a mystery because the father of Ninian and Ransom had accidentally caused the death of the father of Hugo. Guilt about manslaughter and not about seduction has led to Hugo's adoption.

At this sudden return to an earlier situation, Ninian still fights for the money, which Lavinia now claims once again for herself and Hugo. The battle is temporarily suspended by the collapse of Selina, who in this state makes it unhappily clear how much she has been irked by Miss Starkie's endless dissertation on aspects of her own character. The governess attempts to retrieve the situation by assuring her pupils that she has always been good friends with their grandmother, but there is seen to be reason in Ainger's repudiation of the life of a governess when Leah asks. ' "Can people be good friends, when one is despised and rejected by the other?" '

Selina's death does, in the end, prevent the marriage of Hugo and Lavinia. In her will she leaves Hugo a sum of money which will give him the independence he has never had, an increase of fortune which brings him to accept Selina's injunction to abstain from marrying Lavinia. That Lavinia should appear to break the engagement is brought about by the use of Egbert as an intermediary, the woman's privilege of dismissing a fiancé being a point emphasised earlier by the author in *A Father and His Fate*. But Lavinia has learnt the lesson of independence. Unlike Anna Donne (*Elders and Betters*) she has failed in her first attempt to win a husband by purchase, but she refuses a last attempt from Ninian to take over her entire fortune, reserving half for herself in case she needs to make her own life. Unable to shake his daughter's purpose, Ninian retreats to his own room, ordering tea, and a fresh supply of water in five minutes' time. ' "So he feels he is still mighty," said Ainger as he took the jug. "The very minutes stipulated." '

If there is a weakness in *The Mighty and Their Fall* it comes from the departure of Teresa from the centre of the stage, on which her arrival has caused the crisis between Ninian and his daughter. Teresa withdraws to the wings, remarking that she cannot understand why Lavinia saw so much in her father. To which disobliging comment Ninian replies, with natural irritation, that no one should understand better than Teresa. It has been mentioned that Ninian becomes progressively less agreeable as the story proceeds. Lavinia on the other hand becomes more attractive. Even early in the novel she is given a comment which would be an excellent example had Compton-Burnett humour to be represented by a single phrase. Miss Starkie defends her rather suspect educational methods by saying that wild horses would not drag from her any doubts on the subject.

' "Wild horses never have much success," said Lavinia, "Their history is a record of failure." '

Development as a sympathetic character does not, however, protect Lavinia from the emotional ice-age in whose grip the author leaves the Middleton family. Ninian and Teresa are no longer in sympathy. Hugo is shown to care for his comfort more than for Lavinia. Egbert loves his sister, but actively dislikes his father, and has learnt to despise Hugo. As Lavinia says at the time of her fall, when urged by Egbert not to sit alone in her cold room because the sun has gone. ' "Gone for ever," [Lavinia] said, with a smile to make light of her words. "It will not come out again." ' Selina's death, an inescapable disaster, has left her descendants to individual unhappiness. Lonely sadness speaks in the epitaph composed by Agnes, the precocious adolescent daughter. Selina is described only as 'the loving and beloved grandmother of Agnes Middleton'.

After this dying fall it might not have been surprising had Compton-Burnett written in a continuously quieter strain. On the contrary, her subsequent and penultimate novel, the last to be published in her lifetime, is a pyrotechnical display, bursting with literary energy and originality of imagination.

20

PRIAPUS AND HIS POTENTIAL

Unusually for Compton-Burnett, A God and His Gifts opens
with a duologue, a conversation which brings a love affair to
an end. Hereward Egerton makes a final offer of marriage
to Rosa, his mistress, and she refuses him with equal finality,
preferring a single life and the loss of Hereward to a married
life and the loss of her independence. From their exchanges
the reader learns that Hereward is the heir to an estate, that
he is making a name as a writer, that his mother probably
knows of his connection with Rosa, though his father is
unlikely to have remarked on it. An additional circumstance
that has influenced Rosa in her refusal is Hereward's devotion
to his sister, which is rewarded by love and literary assistance.
Hereward does not accept his dismissal without fighting back,
pointing out to Rosa that marriage with him would mean a
fuller life, and geting the devastating reply:
' "I don't want the things it would be full of." '

Refusing to leave her entrenched position, Rosa issues a
warning about the wife, who has been marked down
by Hereward in default of Rosa herself. She knows that
Hereward's sexual needs will not be satisfied by such a
marriage as he contemplates, and she prophesies trouble if he
does not learn restraint, advice hardly likely to be followed
by a self-confessed Priapus such as Hereward. Rosa then passes
from the story, to return only after being in abeyance for
nearly thirty years.

In the Compton-Burnett gallery of baronets, Hereward's father, Sir Michael Egerton has an even greater degree of woolly-headed charm than that possessed by Sir Godfrey Haslam (*Men and Wives*). But Sir Michael is more fortunate than Sir Godfrey in having a wife, Joanna, who can smooth awkward situations, and a butler, Galleon, who cherishes his master, as one who must be protected from a cruel world. Although Galleon has a low opinion of Hereward's literary career, even he admits that money earned in a way unfitted to a gentleman may have its uses. This becomes apparent when Sir Michael is faced with a lawyer's letter, which it requires the united effort of his wife and his butler to induce him to read. Sir Michael is against lawyers. ' "Now what a profession to choose! One that brings trouble and anxiety to innocent people." ' Luckily, matters are not too desperate on this occasion, the letter telling that a parcel of land has been sold for a sum that will reduce Sir Michael's debts to manageable dimensions. Jubilation is, however, cut short by Galleon, who, with the honour of the family at heart, points out that the money raised is a capital sum. In parenthesis, Joanna remarks that it is the smallness of the sums that capital brings in which leads to people getting into debt, but capital itself does not become less, which ' "seems kind and clever of capital" '. Upon this scene, when Sir Michael and his wife are executing a small dance of celebration for a dubious benefit, Hereward and his sister Zillah enter, nipping cheerfulness like a frosty wind. Despairing of convincing his father that it is folly to pay debts from capital, Hereward agrees to undertake the obligation himself, using money earned by what his father can only regard as an absurdly trifling profession. In spite of Zillah's efforts to explain the writer's temperament, her father is far from receptive to the idea that the absent-eyed, unapproachable figure, aloofly accepting meals on trays, is accomplishing anything exceptional.

Having chosen Ada Merton as a suitable wife, Hereward shows no diffidence in proposing to her. He makes his offer in the presence of Ada's father, Alfred, a vaguely donnish widower, her aunt Penelope, a mild duenna, and Ada's sister Emmeline, a minxish girl of sixteen. Hereward also brings his sister Zillah with him, as evidence that he has the support of the member of his family most important to himself. Fortunately for Hereward, the only one of the Mertons free from foreboding at the idea of this marriage is Ada herself, who accepts his offer with enthusiasm. Her father and her aunt feel that she is showing too little regard for the future, while Hereward himself shows an ominous interest in the kittenish Emmeline. Even Zillah privately warns Hereward that he has been too impulsive, but as he insists that only such a marriage could leave his working life with Zillah unaffected, she can argue no more. Charged with breaking the news to her parents, Zillah speaks with such ambiguity that Sir Michael imagines that she is announcing her own engagement to Alfred Merton. He is obliged to change from congratulating a daughter on a prospective marriage to a widower, to giving his blessing to his son's engagement to the widower's daughter. This twist involves Sir Michael in a flurry of words, by which he condones the fact that this is a marriage between long-time acquaintances. ' "We must choose from the people we meet. We hunt in our own demesne . . ." ' Galleon, informed of the engagement by Sir Michael, comments with tepidity on the fact that Ada is said to be proud of Hereward's literary output. ' "I must suppress any personal bias. Sufferance is the badge of all my tribe." '

Sufferance has more demands made on it in the next chapter when Galleon's participation is solicited in the nursery games of the next generation, the three sons of Ada and Hereward. At this moment in the family history Salomon is seven, Merton five, and Reuben a rather wizened three. After ring-a-ring-a-roses has required Sir Michael and Lady Egerton to collapse on the floor, their youngest grandson requests a game of nuts in May. Joanna welcomes Galleon's assurance that no falling down is required in this game, ' "Merely move back and forward in time to the jingle . . ." ', but movement is halted by a family scene. Ada announces that she can no longer tolerate Hereward's far too marked interest in her sister Emmeline. The solution, accepted by all concerned, is banishment for Emmeline. When Hereward recovering from the shock of Ada's attack, tells Zillah that no one will dare to banish her, he finds that she has watched his obsession with Emmeline, and is less startled by Ada's action than he is. Hereward goes so far as to ask what might not he and Zillah been to each other had they not been brother and sister, but Zillah points out that this is a relationship which goes from the beginning to the end. Ada, however, breaks up this conference, and her insistence that she should not be separated from her husband in her own house, is in turn interrupted by the sound of Sir Michael's voice raised in song. He is celebrating Emmeline's banishment by adapting the nursery rhyme that his grandson had asked for. Sir Michael sings about a ' "touch of the frost" ' in 'Nuts in May', 'but that they have managed to smooth it away on "a cold and frosty morning" '.

There is a touch of frost in the next view of the Egerton family, when everyone is ten years older. Satisfied with Salomon's progress, Hereward asks Merton, the second son, how he proposes to make his future, and gets a disturbing answer. Merton is determined to become a writer, but one who will hope to find more fastidious readers than the public commanded by his father. Not unreasonably, Hereward finds exasperation in his son's dismissal of his father's books as intellectually light-weight, but an attempt to change the conversation by talking about Reuben's resemblance to the absent Emmeline leads into deeper waters. Having learnt the reason for her banishment, the boys agree among themselves that they have not really known their father, and that even now there may be more to know.

How much more there is to know becomes apparent when Hereward's sons reach marriageable age, and Hereward enters into competition with them in the sexual arena. It is Merton, still an unpublished author, who brings home the first fiancée. As he says, on announcing his engagement, he is going to hang up his hat in his wife's hall, she being the possessor of a house with a hall, and an income to match. Galleon sees this as a matter for congratulation, relieving Merton from the lowering necessity of making a living by writing. Hetty, Merton's fiancée, takes a more respectful view of literature. She offers admiration to Hereward, who responds with an ominously warm welcome, urging her, as a daughter, to give him her sympathy by visits when he is thought to be working in solitude.

A few weeks later, Merton is faced with the painful need of informing his assembled family that his engagement is broken off, for the not inadequate reason that Hetty is to bear a child of which he is not the father. Merton is suffering so deeply from the idea of losing Hetty that he clutches at Zillah's suggestion that the child might be adopted, and the marriage still take place. Zillah's suggestion is the first step in a discussion as to how the adoption might be arranged, and Ada is gently edged towards the solution that the child should be adopted by Hereward and herself. Oddly enough, the question of adopting a child had been discussed between the husband and wife a few days before, suggested, Ada thinks by Hereward, although he says that he was chiefly interested to gratify his wife's wish to have, once more, a young child in the house. Committed to the plan, Ada becomes uplifted at the idea, undaunted by lack of enthusiasm on the part of

her father. Alfred cannot refrain from strictures on the behaviour of Hetty's seducer, of whom it is only known that he
is married, and is said, by Hereward, to be of ' "our own
class and kind" '. In that case, Alfred points out, the unknown
father has been true to neither, a criticism which Hereward
shows some eagerness to refute. Galleon sees to it that he is
not left out of the secret, but blocks Salomon's attempt to
treat him as a fellow conspirator by saying that he has heard
nothing and so has no need to be sworn to silence, preserving,
in this way, the independence of his own position.

With the portrait of Henry, the child of Hetty and adopted
by Ada and Hereward, the author achieves a final masterpiece of infant delineation. Henry, at three years old,
is stubborn, imaginative to the point of untruthfulness,
acquisitive, and, at moments, movingly tender-hearted. He
has become the centre of the household, but among the devoted circle of grown-ups who vie for his favour, Hereward
is the most doting. Hetty, now married to Merton, and the
mother of a daughter, Maud, has accepted her position in
which her son has been taught to call her ' "Sister Hetty" ',
and can only watch him without making undue demonstra-
tion of affection. She is present when Hereward betrays more
than Hetty's share in Henry's genesis. Spoken half-aloud,
Hereward is overheard by Hetty, by Salomon and by Reuben
to use words of paternal pride.
' "No other [of my children] has been so much blood of my
blood, so deeply derived from me." '
An attempt by Hereward to retrieve his false step by
emphasising Henry's habit of copying everyone is not
accepted by Salomon and Reuben. They have seen that Hetty's
cautious attitude is explained because she lives on the edge
of a precipice, and they have seen that their father grows
careless in his priapic self-confidence. As Solomon says, it
is to be regretted that neither Merton nor his father can

make use of such a dramatic situation in their own writings.

The hidden drama is intensified when Reuben, in his turn, brings home a prospective bride. Reuben has been mildly censured by Galleon for ' "the attempt at schoolmastering . . . a passing phase" ', and it is among his fellow-teachers that he has found Trissie. She matches Reuben in smallness of size, he explains, and her task at school is to teach something called ' "English" ' to the younger boys.

' "Does not she know what it is?" '

"No, or she would be teaching older boys." '

When Trissie arrives to meet her new family, the scene is interrupted by Henry, 'flushed and disturbed', after an encounter with a playful dog at the stables.

' "Bark at Henry! Bite him!" '

"No, no. You know he did not bite."

"He want to. Breathe at Henry. Look at Henry with his eyes." '

This vivid image almost describes Hereward's approach to Trissie, though in asking for sympathetic companionship from this new daughter he gives an assurance that he will ask nothing of Trissie that Reuben, her betrothed, will ' "mind" '. However, Reuben's knowledge of the result of private interviews with his father, leads him to make an appeal that such practices should cease. Hereward is unmoved, considering that his financial aid to Reuben should allow him to spend such time as he chooses alone with Trissie. Insensitiveness and lust get their reward when, failing to influence his father, Reuben hurls his thunderbolt into the family assembly. Hereward fights an unsuccessful rearguard action by suggesting that it is his literary genius that has given some casual words about Henry a meaning beyond the truth, but Reuben kills this fantasy. Merton, called upon for yet another effort of forgiveness, answers an appeal from Salomon not to cut himself off from his father, and his shocked misery seems to draw him closer to Hetty. Sir Michael, kindly and muddle-headed, tells his wife that he wishes he could have spared her this revelation, only to find she has long ago guessed the secret. This has also been the case with Alfred, who shows a reluctance to take Ada back into his home, when his daughter feels that life with such a deceiver has become impossible. Salomon adds his plea that his mother would only be punishing herself by leaving her husband. Zillah, of course, has known everything, and, the reader will recall, Zillah was responsible for planting the idea that Hetty's child should be adopted into the mind of Merton, which has led to Henry's presence as a son of the house.

Henry's own appearance reduces some of the tension. His cheerful greed and jealousy of any mention of little Maud, at once his half-sister and half-niece, distract his soul-wracked relations. These have still another ordeal before them, for as a counter-attack to any analysis of his past actions, Hereward gives the family a stiff talking-to. He has, he says, carried the burden of a man's nature, which has given him the force to serve his own home and to cheer the homes of others. He mentions that, sexually speaking, he is beginning to feel his age, and will be no longer likely to lose his self-control. Reuben has some doubts as to whether this signing-off may be trusted but the priapic apologia meets with the approval of Nurse and Galleon, alert at their listening post in the hall. Galleon goes so far as to say that Hereward has risen above his deplorable profession of writing. Nurse agrees, adding that she has no personal complaint about advances from Hereward. She treats a hint from Galleon that her age, rather than Hereward's self-restraint, may account for her immunity, as a piece of uncalled for coarseness on a delicate subject.

Although this stir-up has little effect on the pattern of the Egerton's family life, it causes Ada to forget the old pain caused her by Hereward's attachment to Emmeline. The idea of having Emmeline, now widowed with an adopted daughter, once more within daily reach, takes a hold on Ada. Indeed it rouses her to biblical fervour— "This my sister was dead and is alive again." ' Recalled to her home, Emmeline is found to have transferred all her interest to her daughter Viola, good-looking and unexpectedly mature for her years. There is a reason for Viola's early development which is not difficult to guess, and which is revealed only too soon. Hereward starts on his old tack of clandestine interviews with an appetising young girl, and this time it is his son Salomon who declares his interest and asks his father to refrain. Hereward replies with a flood of words, to the effect that all the prosperity of the family is due to his exertions and that any temptations yielded to on the way should be set against the importance of Hereward's life's work. Naturally exasperated, Salomon forces out the truth, that Viola is Hereward's daughter by Emmeline, which would, incidentally, account for her appearance being in advance of her supposed age.

The family accept this latest revelation with the *aplomb* they have acquired from past disclosures, but Sir Michael is outraged enough to tell his wife that she must not say that they have yet another grandchild. Joanna, herself, rises to philosophical heights.

' " 'It is a long time ago' people say. So nothing is really wrong. It only has to wait long enough. It is a good thing this has done so." '

When Hereward was destroying Salomon's hope of marrying Viola, he added that he himself has lived unsatisfied, with a want in his heart that Salomon must now feel. The want in Hereward's heart came originally from the refusal of Rosa, his mistress, to marry him, a refusal which has led to all his subsequent entanglements. It is to Rosa that he now returns with a desire for sympathy and a need to extract some material for his next book. Rosa's shrewdness and realism has remained unimpaired by the passing of more than twenty years. She deduces that Hereward's call is made because Salomon has wished to marry Viola, and so Hereward's last secret has been forced from him. She will not accept reproaches that she is at the root of these family tragedies, and retaliates by asking how far Hereward has gone in his private hours with Viola. Along with Rosa, the reader has to accept Hereward's assurance that he has gone no further than he should. ' "Who should have a greater care of her? And I can guard against women's feelings for me." '

Rosa's reply, that he might have put that power to better use, can only be called just. Having failed to extract remorse or regret from Rosa, Hereward does, at least, retrieve a book in which, at the time of his marriage, he has written a poem of farewell, admitting that the theme of his relationship with Rosa is taking literary shape in his mind. He parts from her with the not entirely convincing assurance that her portrait will be unrecognisable. This relationship, Hereward's secret beyond his 'last secret', is now exposed to Ada and Salomon, who happen to find the book and read the poem.

' "Your poor father! I have wondered what he did before we were married. It seems there must have been something."

"Considering what he did afterwards? Yes, there must have been." '

Sir Michael dies, considerately off-stage, and Galleon greets the new baronet with a spattering of ' "Sir Herewards" '. Hereward is uncertain as to his feeling for this new style, but he is firm when Ada praises Joanna's courage, and hopes to do as well when her time comes to be a dowager. Like Mr Bennet in *Pride and Prejudice*, Hereward suggests that his wife is being unnecessarily gloomy, and flatters himself that he may be the survivor. Ada, however, sweeps on, wringing brief and awkward sentences of grief from the company, until as a diversion, Salomon mentions some overdue rents. Hereward says that he has neglected to pass on the rent for Rosa Lindsay, and at this name his last, last secret is revealed to all, even to the fact that Rosa lives rent free. It is Merton who remarks that it is not strange that Hereward admires himself through everything, the oddness lies in doing it openly. It is also Merton who says, ' "There may be breakers ahead," ' when the time comes for Henry to learn the truth about himself. With a final flourish of Olympian defiance, Hereward says that in his hands no harm will come to the younger generation.

At this moment Maud makes her first and only appearance, and there is an opportunity to see if an embryonic, but potentially dangerous affection is growing up between Maud and Henry. Each absorbed in their own drawing, only acknowledging each other in struggles for a pencil, this is the last, but far from least perfect of the author's portraits of children in their relations with each other. Merton still presses his father about Henry's future, and Hereward, rashly, asks Henry who he would like to marry.

' "Dear little Maud," said Henry, in a tone of ending the matter to everyone's content.'

From the excitement of its opening scene to the last words, spoken by the infant Henry and likely to fill his hearers with foreboding, *A God and His Gifts* goes with the swiftness of a train on a scenic railway. To carry the analogy further, the time-lapses between the earlier chapters could be compared to tunnels into which the train passes from sight, to emerge farther down the line still travelling rapidly but with the marks of time on the passengers. Zillah, for example, fades from the possessor of Hereward's every confidence into a background figure with whom he cannot even discuss his ultimate exposure. Ada, on the other hand, becomes ever more formidable as the story proceeds. Even before she begins to speculate on her own behaviour as a widow, she talks with somewhat excessive enthusiasm of the void that will be left by the death of Penelope, her spinster aunt, for many years the usurper of Ada's position with her father. Ada even reaches the point when she is more sympathetic than condemnatory as Hereward's amours are laid bare. Self-condemnation, as Merton points out, is not a feature of Hereward's own character. In his apologia he claims to have ' "cheered the homes of thousands" ', and as a character he has himself the same exhilarating quality.

21

THE LAST BREAKFAST AND
THE LAST BARONET

In 1969, when Dame Ivy Compton-Burnett died, it might have been expected that *A God and His Gifts* would be the last in the inventory of nineteen novels, a list that had begun fifty-eight years before with *Dolores*. By great good fortune Elizabeth Sprigge, a close friend and subsequently a biographer, knew where the twelve exercise books which contained the twentieth novel were to be found. It was also fortunate that Cicely Grieg, who has written her own memorial to the novelist, had become skilled over the years in deciphering a difficult hand-writing and rendering it into typescript. With further assistance from Charles Burkhart, well-known for studies of Dame Ivy's novels, it was found possible to publish a posthumous volume. As a result the reader, though sadly the last time, finds a seat once more at a baronet's breakfast table.

The Last and The First is no exception to earlier books in that the Heriot family is in financial difficulties, which are reflected in the economies in fires and food practised by Eliza, second wife of Sir Robert Heriot. To Hermia and Madeleine, daughters of Sir Robert's first wife, it is a mystery that their father should have married Eliza in any case, and even stranger that he should have made her financial dictator of the family. Eliza cherishes her own children, Angus and Roberta,

230

who, however, have sympathy for the inhibited lives forced on their stepsisters. As an escape from Eliza's nagging self-righteousness, Hermia proposes, financed from the family estate, to take a partnership in a neighbouring girls school, an institution suffering from slackness and deteriorating standards. Although this independent gesture will remove the most rebellious of her subjects, Eliza takes it as a personal insult. Correctly she prophesies that Hermia's skirmishing with her stepmother will be poor training for raising the tone of a wilting school. In practice Miss Murdoch, the head-mistress, finds little difficulty in blocking her partner's attempts at reinvigoration.

This last novel has the quality of a charcoal sketch for an oil painting, with clear outlines, but some of the details more striking than they would be in the finished work. This is particularly to be observed in descriptions of the Grimstone family, neighbours of the Heriots. Mrs Grimstone is a lightly sketched matriarchal type, anxious to cultivate the Heriots as a social leg-up. But her son Hamilton is a portrait in greater depth, and indeed of more weight, flesh having descended on him so as to render him a monument of pendulousness. To his niece Amy his appearance is one for which 'familiarity had had no need to do its accustomed work'. Amy has an elder brother and sister, Osbert and Erica, but as characters they remain embryonic. It is Amy who, attending the school which Hermia Heriot is attempting to reform, suffers tortures of humiliation recalling *Two Worlds and Their Ways*.

Hamilton insists on accompanying his mother to a school concert, at which Amy tries to explain him away as remote relation, tolerated for his contribution to home expenses, a gallant pretence quickly broken down by her school mates. The concert, however, introduces Hamilton to Hermia, and the introduction is followed by a written proposal of marriage. Eliza is so incensed by Hermia's letter of refusal that she does her best to prevent it from being posted. This disappointment to Hamilton is followed by his sudden death (whether or not from being over-weight is not stated). His mother's grief is increased by the discovery that he has left his money to Hermia.

In the meantime the Heriots are making plans to retrench by moving to a smaller house on the estate. Explaining this necessity to Mrs Duff, the housekeeper, leads Eliza into a squabble as to whether the new home is a lodge or a house. Mrs Duff maintaining that 'lodge' is no disgrace ' "when adversity indicates it" '. Hamilton's bequest to Hermia saves the family from the possible opprobrium of living in a lodge, but it also brings about the public humiliation of Eliza. To cover the awkwardness of entertaining the Grimstone family, Madeleine (a descendant of the determined do-gooding spinsters in *Pastors and Masters* and *Parents and Children*) organizes a paper and pencil game. For this purpose she distributes sheets of paper, and, in a scene of great comic charm, finds that the guests have disposed of this material in frivolous ways.

' "May I have another?" said Angus. "I made a rough draft of lines in the middle of mine."

"May I too?" said Amy, glancing at her grandmother. "I began to draw on mine by mistake."

. . . "I must ask for another," said Osbert. "I tore mine up under the mental strain."

"I gave mine to Father," said Roberta, "because he had made his into a hat and could not get it unmade." '

The consequence is that more paper is sought in a seldom-used desk of Hermia's. Among the scrap paper there is a letter of proposal from Osbert to Hermia. It becomes clear that this letter has been suppressed by Eliza, in the fear that its acceptance might cause Hermia to withdraw her contribution to the family finances. As a result of this exposure the marriage takes place, Hermia foregoing her fortune, and with it her full revenge on Eliza. This reversal, paradoxically, creates a friendship between them, and they warm to each other in consultation over the details of Hermia's wedding. Roberta and Angus, discussing the situation agree that Eliza and Hermia have changed roles.

' "How the first can be last, and the last first!" '

These are the last words of the book, and the last words from its author. They sound like the ringing down of a peal of bells, when the arc described grows ever smaller, each note is closer together, until finally the last bell quivers into silence.

In the twenty volumes of her novels, Compton-Burnett created a kingdom over which she ruled absolutely. It is shabby country houses, small country towns, and rambling buildings used for boarding-schools that make up the geography of this kingdom. The dwellers within its frontiers make repeated appearances in different disguises, and so become new characters. They are seldom wicked because they are conventional villains or villainesses but because they suddenly see an opportunity which tempts them to better themselves at the expense of others. Liberty is only achieved when death removes the tyrant, frequently an event long delayed. Children see grown-ups with a distinctness of which the latter are unaware. Servants have a knowledge of their employers' concerns into which it is considered wiser not to probe. School-teachers are judged by their scholars with a sharpened perception that suggests educational methods have not been a failure. It is the variety and richness of these characters, together with the resource and inventiveness of the plots in which they are involved, that make the novels of Dame Ivy Compton-Burnett a living monument to their creator.

Index